Praise

'In this ground-breaking out a comprehensive approach to realising the full potential of companies and the individuals who lead them. He uses evidence to demystify topics such as what makes a truly authentic leader, how to release human potential, the part played by infectious yet grounded optimism, and the impact of personal change and resilience. I have seen his approach in action and have adopted many of his teachings in my own career; as such, I have no hesitation in recommending this outstanding book to anyone interested in improving corporate results and wellbeing.'
— **Guy Munnoch**, Chairman, Hitachi Capital UK PLC and Nedbank Insurance, and adventurer who has summited Everest, trekked to both poles and rowed the Atlantic

'Read this book and you can be better, stronger, faster, happier... The trouble is, it comes at a cost greater than the cover price – that cost is called effort. It's worth the cover price just to find out if you have what it takes. Or you could read an easier book that challenges you less and ultimately makes no difference to your personal happiness and performance!'
— **Adrian Harvey**, entrepreneur, owner and CEO, Elephants Don't Forget, and former managing director, Eon Property Services and British Gas Energy First

'Graham has written an excellent book for business leaders. In essence, any leader who can achieve better mental performance and agility is able to lead more powerfully. This book is a user manual for getting the most from yourself and others in order to create positive change and lasting transformation.'
— **Daniel Priestley**, bestselling author, entrepreneur, and international speaker on entrepreneurship

Graham Keen

Positive Leaders, Positive Change

*Game-changing psychological insights
into maximising profitability and wellbeing*

RETHINK PRESS

First published in Great Britain in 2020 by Rethink Press (www.rethinkpress.com)

© Copyright Graham Keen

All rights reserved. No part of this publication may be reproduced, stored in or introduced into a retrieval system, or transmitted, in any form, or by any means (electronic, mechanical, photocopying, recording or otherwise) without the prior written permission of the publisher.

The right of Graham Keen to be identified as the author of this work has been asserted by him in accordance with the Copyright, Designs and Patents Act 1988.

This book is sold subject to the condition that it shall not, by way of trade or otherwise, be lent, resold, hired out, or otherwise circulated without the publisher's prior consent in any form of binding or cover other than that in which it is published and without a similar condition including this condition being imposed on the subsequent purchaser.

Contents

Introduction	1
PART ONE Positivity And Performance: Modern Psychology's Game-Changing Insights	9
1 Positivity Delivers Competitive Edge	**11**
Evolution and acceptance	13
High-performance states	17
Which comes first: happiness or success?	25
Keep pace with your competition	30
2 Zest Delivers Personal Edge	**35**
Positivity and optimism	36
Resilience	44
Confidence	45
How to get zest	48

3	**Unconscious And Autonomic Game-changers**	**51**
	Perception and reality	53
	One brain, two systems	56
	Action	64
	Learned ownership	69
	Priming	73
	Give your conscious mind a go	75
4	**Powerfully Influencing Followers, Stakeholders And Customers**	**79**
	Grace	80
	Resonance and behavioural style preferences	86
	Scale of impact available through Grace	89
	PART TWO Changing Ourselves	**95**
5	**Cast-iron Personal Change**	**97**
	Why willpower always fails	99
	The self-concept and conditioning	101
6	**Resetting Your Brain's Defaults**	**113**
	Forging pathways in our brains	117
	Mental rehearsal	123
	Emotion accelerates change	131

7 Programmable Self-programming Humans	**133**
Self-talk	134
Correcting self-talk	142
PART THREE The Winning Ethos	**149**
8 Resonant Leadership Mindset	**151**
Leading with Grace	153
Dissonant leadership – and the consequences	157
Leadership stress	161
Profit impact of leadership resonance	167
9 Releasing Discretionary Effort	**169**
Investing in what matters	170
Discretionary effort	172
10 Ethos Change For Exceptional Outcomes	**181**
Leadership, engagement and culture: interlocking facets	183
Remember the substance	186
Beyond empowerment to emancipation	192
Talent – how to get it, hone it and keep it	195
Conclusion	**201**
References	**205**

Acknowledgements	**209**
The Author	**211**
Contact	212

*To my wonderful children, Jamie Keen,
Katy Sands and Bennie Keen*

Introduction

Enlightened business leaders often feel that they must choose between apparently conflicting goals: maximising profitability and showing kindness and respect for those they lead. In fact, there is overwhelming evidence to show that treating people well actually optimises financial performance.

It's easy to think that maintaining a *primary* focus on caring for the wellbeing of employees is a distraction from the wholehearted pursuit of improved financial performance; or even that such 'soft' concerns are an optional nice-to-have, and risk encouraging people to waste time and effort on non-value-adding activities that make no impact on the bottom line. After all, we may be tempted to ask, if we are to attain the highest possible levels of achievement, surely it's obvious that every ounce of effort must be applied to that end?

The fallacy in such thinking is probably obvious: getting an organisational population to contribute to the best of its ability towards that organisation's goals depends on every individual choosing to give their all. This is what we call 'discretionary effort' and it cannot be demanded, exhorted or extorted from people. By definition, discretionary effort is volunteered in response to an individual's internal motivations rather than to the external motivational attempts of others. The leadership task we're faced with comes down to creating an atmosphere in which colleagues choose to contribute optimal discretionary effort. People do that only when they feel a deep emotional engagement with their organisation, its leadership and their immediate bosses.

It is relatively straightforward to engage the efforts of intermediate leaders towards ambitious profit targets, but history teaches us that it's more challenging to engineer a culture in which these managers, and in turn their reports, pursue financial growth in the people-valuing way required to maintain engagement and discretionary effort among colleagues. Manifesting such values consistently and resiliently when we and our teams are under pressure is likely to need widespread positive changes in mindset and behaviour. Despite many corporate leaders' experience being that change is elusive, patchy and short-lived, psychology

INTRODUCTION

has moved on spectacularly in recent years and our ability to create lasting positive change has been transformed. Through new approaches, we can now simultaneously achieve enlightened human values, resilient engagement and stretching profit goals.

My own career has been dedicated to business improvement. I was a senior manager advising entrepreneurs and major clients at Ernst & Young before holding three national and international chief finance officer (CFO) roles. I then spent eight years as an independent corporate finance practitioner in mergers and acquisitions. Shortly after founding my company, New Impetus International, I studied with the father of positive psychology, Professor Martin Seligman, at the University of Pennsylvania to become one of the first five practising positive psychologists in the UK.

It has been my privilege to work in business improvement from two perspectives: finance and psychology – an unusual combination of disciplines. I've accumulated over twenty years' experience, advising more than 200 corporate clients on embedding lasting positive change, and I now work with complex international organisations across Europe, the Middle East and Africa, and beyond, delivering enlightened cultures and financial growth. During this time, I've developed a detailed insight not only into senior corporate leaders' and business owners' issues and objectives, but also into how we can use applied psychology with confidence to implement pragmatic real-world solutions.

I was once challenged by a group of directors, who formed the operational board of a bank, that I was taking through the core New Impetus programme. With perfect justification, they explained that the responsibilities of their senior roles were such that every moment of the working day was packed to the limit with demands on their time. They were less justified in claiming that they had no time to incorporate exercises for managing their own psychology into the daily routine.

This book comprehensively exposes the fallacy in such thinking: managing your own psychology is the key to optimising your personal effectiveness. I was finally motivated to gather up the evidence and write it by the overwhelming weight of recent research that proves the deep congruence and mutual benefits between the bottom line and positive psychology.

My aim is to provide chief executive officers (CEOs) and other C-levels, directors and owners of substantial business units who want to make an even bigger mark in the world with the means to do so through a firmly evidenced approach. That said, the ideas and techniques the book contains are equally relevant for people at earlier stages in their corporate careers. Whatever your role, by creating competitive advantage via congruent goals both for EBITDA and for valuing people throughout the organisation, you will enhance your personal success, career, wealth, happiness and power to make a difference in the world.

INTRODUCTION

There are three evidence-based strands central to creating or fine-tuning step change in your organisation:

1. How and why the behaviour and values that maximise profit put human wellbeing above everything else
2. How leadership behaviour, engagement and cultural actualities combine to become the three inseparable elements of a single ethos
3. How to embed change universally, consistently and reliably, and thereby optimise your *actual* ethos

We'll consider the evidence for this approach and how to use it to deliver superior levels of engagement and profitability. Along the way, we'll overturn common misconceptions and out-of-date beliefs about how to create change and what level of transformation is possible.

Part One shows you how to use contemporary psychology's game-changing insights to optimise the performance of the individual. We'll look at how positive states maximise creativity, resilience, emotional intelligence (EI), analytical reasoning skills, motivation and self-esteem (my CREAMS model). We'll also learn how to defeat depression – which, according to the astonishing statistics, is at any one time probably affecting 19.5% of your colleagues. Finally, we'll examine how to take control of our psychological environment, helping us to default to high-performance states.

Part Two deploys a radical approach to personal change that not only embeds new patterns resiliently in individuals, but also aggregates to deliver your target ethos in the organisation as a whole. We'll examine why the world – and almost certainly your company – is full of people who have tried to make performance and quality of life changes for decades without success and how cognitive restructuring can make such disheartening failure a thing of the past – this is the key to behavioural resilience under pressure. The most successful business leaders and owners are those who embody the ethos they expect their colleagues to share.

Part Three sets out how to embed and sustain a resonant leadership mindset, emotional engagement and enlightened corporate culture: the key elements of an optimal ethos. We'll consider the practicalities of dealing with the challenges that inevitably come up in the real world:

- Does it matter if one of your reports occasionally falls into an autocratic leadership style short of resonant leadership?

- What elements of engagement actually make a difference to discretionary effort?

We'll look at the answers to these and other knotty questions, and draw on evidence to understand the core factors. We'll also pause briefly to explore the fundamental difference between the cultural values expressed in mission statements and the like, and the values that the people in an organisation actually manifest. It will become clear how futile it is to invest in communicating (again!) the values people already know about and aspire to, but do not manage to adopt, instead of promoting activity and interventions that will actually help people to change their behaviour.

The material in this book is the basis of the method my company has developed with thousands of delegates over twenty-four years into a routine that's compatible with demanding lifestyles. Once you put it into action, this approach will rapidly start to deliver the personal changes that you and those you lead decide to target. Alongside this, research has shown it increases happiness, success, financial freedom, career profile and wellbeing. Personal changes in your followers and colleagues then aggregate across the organisation as a whole, as cultural engagement and financial performance improve. This inevitably creates competitive advantage for both the corporation and your people. All of this gives you the capacity to make more of a difference in the world, so that it matters even more that you were here.

PART ONE

POSITIVITY AND PERFORMANCE: MODERN PSYCHOLOGY'S GAME-CHANGING INSIGHTS

Though positive psychology as a discipline is relatively young, it has transformed our thinking about what human beings are capable of in all areas of life. Harnessing positivity as a way to enhance our engagement with others delivers exceptional outcomes.

ONE
Positivity Delivers Competitive Edge

Drawing on the wealth of research that has taken place since positive psychology as a discipline began in the late 1990s, I'm confident in saying that we now know enough about positivity to justify prioritising it, arguably above all else, in developing a corporation and building a life.

Positivity and happiness are intimately and inextricably linked. Indeed, happiness is often defined by psychologists as experiencing positive emotions. Professor Barbara Fredrickson, widely regarded as the leading authority in this area, lists the main positive emotions as joy, gratitude, serenity, interest, hope, pride, amusement, inspiration, awe and love.[1] In thousands of studies involving hundreds of thousands of people, positivity in its various forms has been shown to improve our relationships, creativity, resilience, intelligence, emotional skills, motivation, wellbeing, earnings, careers, productivity, sales, leadership effectiveness – the list is almost endless.[2]

And no summary of the benefits of positivity is complete unless it includes health. There is incontrovertible evidence on the benefits of happiness and positivity for maintaining health and mobility post-retirement, longevity (optimists have an additional nine years' life expectancy), lowering blood pressure, strengthening immune systems, increasing tolerance of pain and preventing clinical depression, where the difference is a staggering 88%.[3]

In business, we tend to think of positivity more as a mindset or mental attitude than a set of feelings. It's clearly both, because it has been shown time and again that negative emotions in the moment destroy our positive outlook.

A positive person is always going to be looking at the upside, at the seeds of opportunity among the shards of something that hasn't worked out. They not only

---

1   B Fredrickson, *Positivity* (Crown Publishing Group, 2009), p39
2   S Lyubomirsky, L King and E Diener, The benefits of frequent positive affect: Does happiness lead to success? *Psychological Bulletin,* 131 (2005) 803–855, p834; see also S Achor, *The Happiness Advantage* (Crown Publishing Group, 2010), p41
3   M Seligman, *Authentic Happiness: Using the new positive psychology to realize your potential for lasting fulfillment* (Simon & Schuster, 2002)

project positivity, they also *consume* it. They are not in stasis, rather they are in a dynamic relationship with their environment, pushing positivity out to other people and into situations at the same time as they gather it in from what's going on around them.

Positive people simply notice more of the positives because of a specific property of the brain that we'll examine in Chapter 3. All people notice really important positive things; positive people also notice secondary, or less critical, positive things that negative people miss. They are primed for success and – that magical quality in work teams – solutions-oriented.

Evolution and acceptance

Since I first started getting professionally involved in positivity twenty-five years ago, I've seen a huge shift in public attitudes, from doubt and disbelief to acceptance and enthusiasm. I believe the change is still gathering momentum: positivity, wellbeing and people-centred values are now in fashion, so it's puzzling that so many people in the workplace either openly contest the power of positivity, or do not reflect such an approach in their behaviour.

I face this attitude on a regular basis when starting to work with a new group. Sometimes people just don't engage with the process I'm taking them through; at other times they will openly challenge me.

'We're all earning over a million a year – what makes you think you have anything to teach us?' said a cynical director at one well-known professional services firm. Then there's the company joker, trying to undermine the process by shouting out inappropriate jokes or taking the piss. I also come across people who think there's something unique about their psychology that means they're the one human being on the planet for whom positivity won't work. Really?

Whatever is driving these misinformed objections – insecurity, fear of change, intellectual conviction, need for power or control – I've found that there is one surefire way to overcome them: evidence. Clearly it helps to demonstrate that positivity adds value in a business by improving outcomes from engagement to EBITDA. It's also reassuring to learn that all humans are capable of radical change, and that the reason for our past failure to change is simply to do with strategy. And people need to know that pursuing a positive mindset isn't going to turn them into someone else, just into a happier and more effective version of themselves.

Partly because of my CFO past, I'm interested in sales performance, and anything that's good for revenue gets my attention. But I'm also an admirer of salespeople. They are our brave colleagues who must push through rejection, disappointment, discourtesy and even derision every single day. We would not survive without their courage and resilience – in most cases, we would not be able to exist at all without them. It's no surprise to me that the best sales professionals are positive: positive salespeople outperform negative salespeople by 56%.[4] A 2006 study proved that a positive mindset in negotiations leads to both a more efficient process and a more successful outcome.[5] Other studies have shown that a salesperson who is adept at triggering positive emotions in their client or prospect will outperform others by 123% and at least 500% in conquest and account sales respectively.[6]

Positive leaders, particularly those who invest their focus on creating positive reactions in the people they lead as well as in themselves, are far and away the most effective leaders. This reciprocal positivity, which I call 'Grace', has been shown to be the most important factor in determining how a CEO's financial results compare to those of their peers.

POSITIVITY IMPROVES PROFIT

The regime Melanie inherited when she became MD of a niche financial services firm was based on a pessimistic approach to business and an autocratic management style. Having attended my core programme years earlier, she was a fervent believer

---

4 Achor, *The Happiness Advantage*, p15
5 S Kopelman, AS Rosette and L Thompson, The three faces of Eve: Strategic displays of positive, negative, and neutral emotions in negotiations. *Organizational Behavior and Human Decision Processes*, 99:1 (2006), pp81–101
6 S Sloan and LM Spencer, Participant survey results. Hay Salesforce Effectiveness Seminar, Atlanta GA (Hay Group, 1991)

in the power of positivity to transform financial performance, and she felt that the current company culture was inhibiting it.

We discussed whether everyone in the leadership team, and in the business as a whole, would embrace a positive business ethos and decided to give them the chance to do so. I worked initially with the extended leadership team to increase their positivity and resilience. I also set out the evidence supporting enlightened human values in leadership as the way to improve engagement and financial performance. Melanie was a committed champion and exemplar, and the leadership team worked wholeheartedly on embedding the new positive culture.

We then extended the programme to everyone within the business. Melanie defined the new culture, and again buy-in was almost universal. Alignment with the new values now forms part of every leadership meeting and employee performance review. People talk about the transformation they have experienced in both their professional and personal lives, and about the enjoyment and fulfilment they experience as a result.

The company is now performing substantially above target and has the highest engagement scores in the holding company group. Despite adverse market conditions, its revenue growth is so strong (over 25%) that Melanie has further increased the revenue and EBITDA targets she is setting for next year.

High-performance states

In Chapter 8, we're going to look in detail at how leaders make this approach work and how to emulate their success. For now, I want to focus on the fact that such leaders generate positive emotional states in themselves and others.

The reason this gives them extra impetus is that positive states are high-performance states. Positive states deliver significant improvements in six main areas: creativity, resilience, EI, analytical reasoning skills, motivation and self-esteem (aptly summarised in the acronym CREAMS). Four of these areas deliver benefits in real time; two of them build improvement over time.

Creativity and solution finding

Whenever I ask a class or an audience how often in their business lives they are required to show creativity, they always have the same response: daily, often continuously. In fact, it's every time they refine a process, design a proposal, solve an issue, devise a strategy or seek to influence a stakeholder.

Like all higher functions, creative skills are a property of the cerebral cortex, which functions best when we are relaxed, positive and free from negative emotions. The ultimate relaxed, fully conscious state is when our brainwaves are in alpha pattern, which happens, for example, on the cusp between sleep and wakefulness.

But when stress goes above the tipping point, the limbic system and the pre-frontal cortex jointly close down the cerebral cortex, blocking all higher functions completely – including the capacity to generate creative solutions. This reaction shows how futile it is to put pressure on people we want to create ideas or design solutions. You may have heard it described as the 'fight, freeze or fly' response, or more likely 'fight or flight'.

It means that control of our actions has been returned to the simplest part of the brain – our reptile brain – which can only handle a very small number of options. This enables us to take decisions instantly, which gives us the best chance of survival when confronted by a sudden existential threat. If our higher functions were still in control of decisions, we would have a much larger thought/action repertoire to sift through before deciding on the appropriate response. That fraction of a second's delay could mean the difference between surviving and not, so this capacity has been favoured by natural selection.

Many of our greatest innovators throughout history have used super-relaxed states to bring their creativity to full power. René Descartes spent his mornings in bed, meditating on his current theory; Albert Einstein sat in quiet reverie and conducted his 'thought experiments'– visualisations of the problem he was working on; and Thomas Edison had a favourite chair where he 'sat for ideas' while he held a brass sphere in each hand, poised over brass preserving pans on the floor. As he dozed off, the spheres fell into the pans, waking him up, and he would immediately write up the insights he'd had while his mind was in this relaxed and fertile state. Both Winston Churchill and Salvador Dali developed their own version of Edison's technique. I encourage you to try it.

Resilience

Time spent in positive states brings about synaptic and biochemical changes in the brain that build resilience. For all of us, the more time we spend in positive states, the greater our resilience. This doesn't mean we're resilient when we're happy – someone who is feeling upbeat but lacks resilience is quickly derailed when circumstances change for the worse. It just means that optimistic people, because they spend more time in positive states, are more resilient. We'll explore resilience further in Chapter 2.

Consider the impact on your business if all of your colleagues were more resilient. No one would be easily deflected from the shared purpose or discouraged by adverse conditions, still less give in to the temptation to seek the haven of unjustified sick leave. No one would give up at the first or even repeated rejection.

Everyone would just keep on doing what needs to be done until the goal is achieved.

Whether at work, home or play, resilient people stay calm, strong and purposeful for everyone else when stuff hits the fan.

Emotional intelligence

EI is one of the most important characteristics in business. It is at the heart of any human interaction where getting the desired outcome depends on influencing others successfully: for example, leadership, shareholder and press relations, marketing, sales, customer service, teamwork and cross-functional collaboration.

EI is our awareness of our own emotional states and those of others, and our ability to manage our impact on both. It's entirely dependent on us being in a positive state; just as with creativity, above a certain tipping point, negative states like anxiety, stress, anger or jealousy close down this part of our brain's functionality.

In a positive state, we are naturally aware of others' emotions; in a negative state, we are blind to them and don't really care – we are too taken up with our own issues. Just think of the reactions you get from a person in a negative state, for example, hacked-off waiters and shop assistants, disengaged or overstressed colleagues.

Analytical reasoning skills

How much of our analytical intelligence is available to us at any given moment is governed to a large extent by our emotions. It's axiomatic that high intelligence results in superior effectiveness, which inevitably translates into improved business performance. Indeed, one study showed that above-tipping-point IQ in CEOs is associated with 50% higher business unit profits than average.

Positive emotional states leave the cerebral cortex fully engaged, so enable us to deploy all of our intellect. They engender positive expectations, which accelerate the rate at which we find solutions. Equally, we make better decisions when we're positive, and are well advised to defer making a judgement until we are sure we have achieved a positive state.

Negative emotions diminish our analytical reasoning skills. For example, although a little stress gives us an edge, once we get to our tipping point (which, for most of us, is quite low), our abilities retreat quite quickly. Look at the injudicious things people say when they are angry and frustrated, hurting the one they love, or insulting the boss on whom their future depends. Furthermore, negative emotional flooding, for example an emotional hijack like losing our temper, inhibits our intelligence for up to eight hours while the stress hormones dissipate.

Motivation

Positive emotional states deliver high motivation – we know how easy it is to hit the gym or make that tough phone call when we are feeling happy and positive. Conversely, negative states (bored, sad, lonely) totally destroy motivation. At the risk of stating the obvious, high motivation creates high productivity, minimises procrastination and reduces avoidance of tough issues – it's a factor in both revenue and profitability.

One of the many ironies of our social evolution outstripping our biological evolution is that exactly when we need our motivation, it deserts us. You're likely to be able to think of many examples of not being motivated to do the very thing that's absence is the cause of your malaise, eg exercising or calling someone.

It's an evolutionary trait: in human pre-history, it was often safer to hide in a deep, dark hole than confront whatever was causing distress, like a predator attacking the group. The ones who hid survived more often, so that trait was selected in by evolution.

In passing, I want to touch on a couple of misconceptions you may have come across:

- Don't be fooled by the SOB paradox. Some who wield negative motivation may succeed, but research tells us two things:

- They would do even better to be positive; they only get away with it because of their massive talent and drive.
- Their impact is always mitigated by positive lieutenants who mop up the emotional detritus they leave behind.[7]

* Studies have long proven that, although both negative and positive motivation work:
  - Positive works better.
  - *Only* positive brings about lasting behaviour change.

Self-esteem

Self-esteem is about our unconscious opinion of ourselves, our beliefs about our personality and skills, how much we value ourselves and how much we believe others should value us. High self-esteem manifests in a wide range of charismatic and highly effective behaviours. These include confidence, humility (arrogance is a compensation behaviour born out of low self-esteem), owning mistakes, accepting criticism on merit and focusing on others above self. It's an essential component of influencing skills (see Chapter 4 on Grace), particularly in leadership and in

---

[7] D Goleman, R Boyatzis and A Mckee, *Primal Leadership: Realizing the power of emotional intelligence* (Harvard Business School Press, 2002), pp80–83

reaching our full potential at work, home and play. Unsurprisingly, it's a profit- and revenue-enhancing factor in business.

Self-esteem is predominantly a learned attribute that is unconsciously self-programmed into us over our lifetime. No one can have too much of it, and we can all acquire more via cognitive conditioning (see Chapter 7). It is built when we are engaged in the sincere (private, internal and humble) self-praise and savouring of our successes and strengths that happens more in optimistic people.

Positive people notice more about themselves that is praiseworthy and they don't feel the need to dodge it – they accept it on merit. Negative or pessimistic people are more likely to reframe the good as atypical or temporary. Self-esteem is reduced and damaged by such fault-finding self-analysis and rumination.

The more time we spend in positive states, the more optimistic we become, the more our wholesome self-esteem grows and the better our performance – which is not surprising since we will be giving free rein to our CREAMS.

We all have to remember what the evidence tells us. Positivity is no longer a nice-to-have, it's a must-have if you want to compete as an organisation, achieve your full potential as a leader, and maximise your happiness, wellbeing and success as an individual at home, work and play.

The important thing to remember is that we are not helpless about how much positive emotion we experience; there's a lot we can do to increase it. Increased optimism and hope are the key, because optimists experience more positive emotion by definition. Happily, optimism and pessimism are not simply traits we inherit, they are largely behaviours we learn. In Part II, we will look at how to embed the optimism, hopefulness and positivity we choose.

Which comes first: happiness or success?

The feelings of pleasure and achievement we experience when we reach a goal or complete a project successfully, or turn in financial performance ahead of budget, have led to widespread misconceptions about which comes first: happiness or success. In these examples, the success event precedes the emotion, so it's natural for us to assume that the success caused happiness. There is no denying that success can lead to a whole range of positive emotions: joy, elation, excitement and – yes – happiness. But it is now well established by an impressive number of studies that success alone far from guarantees happiness.

POSITIVITY, HAPPINESS AND PERFORMANCE: THE EVIDENCE

Success in many facets of life is associated with happiness. In 2005, three leading lights of positive psychology undertook a meta-analysis of 225 research studies, which between them had 275,000 participants, to determine whether happiness creates success.[8]

The original assumption was that it was the other way round – that success caused happiness – and indeed there was some evidence for this, but the meta-analysis clearly demonstrated 'directional causality'. In other words, happiness caused success in a long list of domains, including marriage and relationships, income, work, business, community involvement, health, energy, originality and longevity.

In his book *The Happiness Advantage*, Harvard researcher Shawn Achor emphasises this: 'Data abounds showing that happy workers have high levels of productivity, produce higher sales, perform better in leadership positions, and receive higher performance ratings and higher pay… Happy CEOs are more likely to lead teams of employees who are both happy and healthy, and who find their work climate conducive to high performance.'[9]

---

[8] Lyubomirsky et al, The benefits of frequent positive affect
[9] Achor, *The Happiness Advantage*, p41

Although success feels great, it is neither necessary nor sufficient to ensure happiness, which is a deeper, more fulfilling and less ephemeral emotion than mere pleasure. Happiness is also more complex. There is no absolute consensus in positive psychology as to its precise definition. This is partly because positive psychologists think about happiness differently from the general public, who don't need to define it, they just know what it feels like.

We've known for a while that the assumption that the pursuit of happiness is the fundamental human motivator is wrong. Ivan Maslow famously clarified our thinking on that in the 1950s and 1960s with his Hierarchy of Needs. But Western society still maintains its fascination with happiness. Seligman's generally accepted theory, which has stood up well to being tested over twenty years of research studies, is that when we're free from coercion of any kind, what human beings seek is wellbeing, of which happiness is just a part.[10]

Wellbeing comprises five elements: positive emotions, engagement (in this context meaning flow), fulfilling relationships, meaning and accomplishment. Positive psychology was founded as the science of maximising human wellbeing, not just happiness. Researchers in this area tend to equate happiness with positivity or positive emotions, and most of them say happiness is

---

10 M Seligman, *Flourish: A new understanding of happiness and well-being – and how to achieve them* (Nicholas Brealey, 2011), p9

a combination of positive emotion, engagement and meaning.

So which does come first? Hundreds of studies have now demonstrated that in areas ranging from marriage and friendship, through health and career, to community and commerce, happiness leads to success. I want to emphasise that there isn't merely a correlation between happiness and success – that would prove nothing except that the one is associated with the other. Naysayers love to jump on the difference between correlation and causality in an attempt to discredit research that makes them uncomfortable because it undermines their negative opinions, but research scientists in general and positive psychologists in particular are acutely aware of the fundamental difference between correlation and causality. This is why they design their studies meticulously to go beyond correlation and discover the direction of causality: happiness causes success.

The final word on this subject, however, goes to neither happiness nor success, but to positivity. It turns out, as I'm sure many people would regard as self-evident, that positivity creates happiness. Indeed, many positive psychologists use the concepts of happiness, positivity and positive emotions interchangeably.

It's important to make the distinction between positive thinking and positivity. Positive thinking includes, and in some people's minds, consists solely of, a positive mental attitude, ie consciously choosing to reframe events in a constructive and positive light. While this is undoubtedly immensely valuable in conditioning us towards positivity, it's not the same thing.

The keyword is 'consciously': positivity is the unconscious experience of positive emotions, and although a positive mental attitude can become a person's unconscious automatic default, it's not a prerequisite for positive thinking. In other words, positive thinking can be a correction of a person's natural negative response to a situation. That's a good thing, but not as good as genuine positivity, where our responses are naturally positive.

Finally, positive thinking and Pollyanna thinking are two different things. Pollyanna thinking encourages people to pretend that bad things are good, not by reframing, just by lying to themselves. If someone had a road accident and broke their arm, Pollyanna thinking would say, 'Hooray! I've broken my arm,' whereas positive thinking might reframe the situation by saying, 'Thank goodness I survived.' In psychological terms, Pollyanna thinking adds no value, and can in fact be extremely unhelpful, even damaging. As we will see in Chapter 7 on self-talk, attempting to condition ourselves by deploying obvious untruths simply does not work.

The thing to focus on in the pursuit of success is positivity. This doesn't mean forcing ourselves to be positive when everything in our psychology wants to be negative – ultimately, such self-discipline-based approaches cannot succeed. Rather, genuine positivity is where we automatically and unconsciously default to being positive. That inevitably generates happiness and results in success.

The fantastic news is that genuine positivity is a learned behaviour, and as such can be conditioned into our unconscious responses. The method is beautifully simple: positives in, positives out. To increase our genuine positivity, we need to take control of the conditioning we allow into our brains and make sure that the vast majority of it is positive.

Keep pace with your competition

When I first started out as a psychologist in 1997, the discipline of positive psychology had not yet begun, neurobiology was still experimenting with neuroplasticity and the concept of applied EI was new. The evidence we all now take for granted linking positivity and corporate performance did not exist. Fuelled by the outlandish claims of mid-century positive thinking adherents, widespread scepticism prevailed in the corporate world about mind-brain science. All of this gave early adopters of the emerging knowledge a real performance advantage.

A TALE OF TWO GOLFERS

In 1998, a colleague and I were working as sports psychologists with one of the top-five Tour-professional golfers in Europe, who turned out to be an eager early adopter of the positive psychology and neurobiology breakthroughs happening at that time. He was completely dedicated to what we were sharing with him, and it gave him a real edge over the competition, who were as yet ignorant of what could be achieved. As a result, he more than doubled his winnings in the following season, shooting up in the world rankings as a result.

Eight years later, I was working with another talented Tour pro: a young man with impressive statistics in the amateur game. The manager of our 1998 client was also his manager, and considered him to be just as good a ball striker, but he was not finding the transition into the professional game easy. In the amateur game, he could rely on his raw talent to rise to the top, but competition on the European Tour is of a higher order of magnitude. He was finding motivation a real challenge.

We worked together on exactly the same material as we had in 1998, updated by the intervening eight years of research. Sadly, this golfer could not bring himself to make the effort needed to master the new psychology, and we parted company. He went on to lose his playing rights and dropped out of the European Tour for some years.

The contrast is stark: in 1998 one exceptionally talented pro used sports psychology to gain competitive advantage over other top players in the world and achieve global success. In 2006, another pro, who was also more talented than 95% of the pros on the Tour, decided not to adopt sports psychology, and was then not even able to keep up with lesser players who were using it. By 2006, sports psychology was mainstream and the majority of Tour pros were using it. Nowadays, 100% of them use it.

The situation in business psychology is analogous. Exactly as with sports psychology from 1998 to 2006, things are now completely reversed. The evidence has been out there for some time and most business leaders are at least aware of it. Positive cultures have been part of how conspicuous market disruptors have broken the mould. Middle management take it for granted that treating people well and caring for their happiness and wellbeing are essential.

In fact, the days of positivity giving you a cast-iron competitive advantage are numbered. It is fast becoming a *must-have* just to keep pace with the competition. Assume your competitors are doing everything they can to exploit the enormous potential of individual psychological development described in this book. Unless a company is on top of this area, they now risk losing their playing rights, just like my 2006 golfing client, the equivalent in business being for a company to find itself a target rather than an acquirer.

There is still time – not every board room has bought in yet. No one knows how long that will last, but consider this: in 2000, when I founded my company, no one had heard of mindfulness, and most business leaders regarded techniques like visualisation as unproven at best. Now when I meet a new class of middle managers and ask for a show of hands as to who in the room has knowledge and experience of mindfulness and visualisation, I get a 90% positive response. Future senior leaders are all over this.

TWO
Zest Delivers Personal Edge

In one of my first substantial assignments, I was asked by the MD of a division of a global insurance major to improve the success of his division. He explained that his was already a high-performing business unit full of highly capable professionals, but he felt strongly that they were capable of even more if we could add something to their mindset that he called 'zest'. The idea took root in my psyche, and now I use zest to describe the behaviour and thinking that make up a fantastic high-performance way of being.

The reason why I put so much emphasis on zest in everything my team and I do and try to bring more zest into the lives of everybody that we work with is because it gives such advantages in terms of quality of life and outcomes at both a business and personal level.

Zest is both a mindset and a culture, comprised of four major areas: positivity and optimism, motivation, resilience, and confidence. Though we covered some of these areas in the previous chapter, there is more we need to consider in relation to the individual's positivity and optimism, resilience, and confidence.

Positivity and optimism

When my team and I are working with people to improve their happiness, we often ask them to focus on positive emotions in relation to three aspects of their lives: their past, their present and their future. We can use this approach to deepen our understanding of what genuine positivity means to them and how we can help them make small changes for lasting improvement.

Positivity about the past

The things that have happened to us in the past are continuously popping back into our mind and informing the way that we perceive current events. If a person has had a lot of negative experiences and associated negative feelings, that negativity is constantly being brought into the present tense and changing how they experience what's going on in their *current* life. They then find it harder than somebody with a lot of positive events in their past to interpret the present in a positive light.

Crucially, it is not the nature of the event itself that determines how we experience it; it is how we *perceive* the nature of it. Finding ways of tidying up our memories so that we can be open to positivity is a big part of making sure that our current efforts for the present and future are given the best opportunity to succeed.

For a lot of people, positivity about the past is challenging. We need to see the whole of our past in a positive context, yet by the time we've been on the planet for a few decades, most of us have experienced things about which it's not easy to feel upbeat. Developing genuinely positive feelings about the past can require a lot of effort, and may even require professional therapy, for example to deal with trauma.

Positive psychology has achieved epoch-making breakthroughs with techniques that help us improve how we feel about things in the past. Two of these have received much attention as interventions that add value in the corporate setting: forgiveness and gratitude.

Psychologists consider forgiveness in this context to be an entirely internal act: we're forgiving someone who's made us unhappy in the past privately and secretly for ourselves, as a way of getting out from under the negative influence of the memories of what happened and what went wrong. The person we are forgiving need not, and indeed in most cases should not, know about it.

In countless studies, gratitude has been shown to be associated with a long list of benefits, including increased energy levels, reduced risk of anxiety and depression, being more forgiving, humbleness, motivation and wellbeing.[11] For this reason, it is receiving growing attention from positive psychology researchers.

> ### REFRAMING
>
> Finding a way of reframing things that have happened to you in the past makes an important contribution to delivering genuine positivity in the present. Ask yourself, 'How can I think about this differently?'
>
> Next time you tell a story about your past, to yourself or others, take the opportunity to boost your positivity in the present. I'm not saying you should make it up; I'm suggesting you look for the most positive aspects of the narrative, for example, academic setbacks that your current occupation shows you have overcome; a rift with a friend or family member with whom you are now on good terms; business challenges you have triumphed over.

Positivity about the present

Genuinely positive people are predisposed to seeing the positive in every situation. They are not in stasis;

---

[11] See, for example, RA Emmons, *Thanks! How the new science of gratitude can make you happier* (Haughton Miffin, 2007)

they are in a vibrant, dynamic relationship with their environment, in which they project positivity to other people and into situations *whi*le they draw in positivity from what's going on around them.

Their unconscious expectation is that the world is going to present them with a lot of positives. They are, if you like, primed for opportunity and can't help but home in on the positive stuff in their environment. They are solutions-oriented. Everyone notices the stuff that's dangerous or really important. Positive people also notice the secondary positive stuff.

> **SAVOURING**
>
> Notice how you experience your day-to-day life. Focus on looking for the best in every situation, good or bad. Consciously savour your achievements and environment. Give yourself even more opportunities to feel positive about things as they happen. Prime yourself for positivity through your choice of language and observations.

Positivity about the future

Optimism is being positive or happy about the future. My preferred definition is 'expecting positive outcomes'.

Psychologists call someone's position on the optimism/pessimism spectrum their 'explanatory style', because it defines how they explain the world to themselves. Although human beings share a genetic predisposition towards pessimism (see below), where we end up on the optimism/pessimism spectrum is a conditioned, or learned, response based on how we have mentally processed our life experiences. I must emphasise again that it's not the life experiences themselves, but how we process them that shapes our explanatory style.

This was graphically illustrated by a *World in Action* programme, decades ago, which considered the life outcomes of two brothers. They were close in age and their life chances were, on the face of it, not promising: their father was a recidivist criminal with alcohol and drug issues, and prone to domestic violence. One brother turned out very similar to his father, which he explained as being inevitable, since he saw himself as trapped by his father's nature. The other qualified as a solicitor and became a partner in a firm of lawyers, which he said was a direct result of his upbringing: he felt he had no choice but to work hard to escape it. The two brothers processed identical circumstances very differently, arising from explanatory styles at opposite ends of the spectrum and resulting in completely different outcomes.

Our genetic susceptibility to negativity and pessimism is sometimes ascribed to the Pleistocene brain, so called because it evolved during the Pleistocene epoch, when our distant forebears were more likely to survive if they expected danger at every turn. Not only has this resulted in roughly 70% of humans being pessimistic, but it also means that our response to negative events is much stronger than our response to positive ones. Indeed, our brains are hardwired to seek out and respond to negatives, but to pay much less attention to positives, largely taking them for granted. It has been estimated that a negative event has two to five times the impact on us of a positive event of equal strength.

The behavioural impact of this predisposition is immense and almost infinitely far-reaching. All we have to do is think for a moment about the effect of our brains emphasising and spotting negatives at the same time as undervaluing and ignoring the positives. Consider the contribution this makes in politics, personal relationships and so on.

For our present purposes, let's focus briefly on how it influences leaders and colleagues to respond to opportunities and threats in the commercial environment: it's almost inevitable that we underestimate the former and exaggerate the latter. You might be tempted to think that sounds like a safe approach; if so, that's your Pleistocene brain at work. The point is that such evaluations are skewed towards pessimism and lose the objectivity successful business leaders strive for.

We tend to have strong, frequently unflattering opinions about people whose explanatory style conflicts with our own. Optimists generally like to celebrate early, believe that people on the whole are helpful, and see setbacks and negative events as the exception to the rule. Pessimists don't like to tempt fate, know the world to be full of people who will take advantage of them and view negative events as the norm. More often than not, our mutual accusations turn out to be factually incorrect.

Not all pessimists are inappropriately negative: for example, it's helpful for a lawyer to anticipate everything that can go wrong so they can protect their client. And optimists don't just bury their heads in the sand; they are in fact much more likely than pessimists to seek the true facts, because their higher resilience means they are psychologically better able to handle disappointment. Pessimists, on the other hand, experience greater discomfort with disappointment. As it's hardwired into all humans to avoid discomfort, pessimists are more prone to unconsciously dodging potentially uncomfortable truths – even though they then go on to obsess about them when they cannot be avoided.

The issue here is not which group is right, but which explanatory style leads to a statistically higher probability of happiness, superior financial performance and personal success. In fact, it is reasonable to argue that both styles are correct, because they are consistent with the way the individuals concerned experience the world. Importantly, the evidence overwhelmingly supports optimism as the route to profitability and wellbeing. Fortunately, as we have seen, explanatory style is predominantly a learned mindset, and as such we are able to change it when we want to.

Because of the benign world view it engenders, optimism leads to more intense and more frequent positive emotional states, whereas pessimism naturally increases the intensity and quantity of negative states like anxiety and fear, suppressing positive states like joy and elation.

LANGUAGE

Making a small change to the language you choose can have a marvellous impact on your optimism. When you think about future events, always describe them to yourself in positive terms. Get into the habit of thinking about the opportunities that are coming your way. If you are blocked by a feeling of fear or nervous anticipation, it's OK to acknowledge this, but do so in positive terms. Then talk or think your way through how you will overcome the obstacles you foresee: 'Yes, it will be challenging to achieve this target by that date, but I know we can do it because we have the time to prepare and the skills within the team to make it happen.'

Reframing future events like this will prime your brain to look for the opportunities to succeed.

Resilience

We know resilience as the ability to push through potential setbacks rather than be deflected by them, and to maintain our momentum towards the outcome we desire. Resilience also comprises two further qualities that support our drive towards our goals: grit and emotional stability.

Grit

There has been a lot of research on grit in the positive psychology movement in recent years, particularly by the brilliant Angela Duckworth.[12] Grit is the ability to sustain interest and effort towards your long-term goals. It's a resource that's much more readily available to people who spend large amounts of time in positive emotional states.

Resilience and grit are a huge part of zest. It's obvious that if you manage to sustain your interest and your effort towards goals that are important to you, then you're much more likely to achieve them – *and* you're much more likely to have a good time while you're doing so.

---

12   A Duckworth, *Grit: The power of passion and perseverance* (Simon & Schuster, 2016)

Emotional stability

Emotional stability has significant implications for all our relationships, whether at work or at home. Effectiveness as an influencer, for example, whether in sales, leadership or team membership, depends on it. Somebody who's highly emotionally stable will maintain their positive emotional state in the face of opposition that would deflect other people, turning them from feeling happy, confident and energetic to feeling discouraged or depressed.

When you're deflected from a positive emotional state into a negative one by some setback – be it large or small – you fall out of a high-performance state into a low-performance one. All of your CREAMS are adversely affected when this happens.

Confidence

Confidence is one of the most universally sought-after improvements in individual mindset and a resource we all sometimes wish we had more of. There are three aspects to this prized quality.

Faith in ourselves

What we think about most often in relation to confidence is our faith in ourselves. Confidence is our belief in our ability to be the person we want to be, to achieve the things we've set ourselves to achieve and to handle all of our responsibilities in any situation we are likely to meet – and especially our belief that we can do this *right now*.

People who have enormous faith in their ability to deal with those things tend not to be distracted by worrying about whether they're going to be able to 'pull this off', or whether they're going to be comfortable, effective, pleasant, likeable or make a positive contribution. People with the right level of confidence simply get on with doing what needs to be done, so their attention is focused outward, towards other people rather than in on themselves.

The relationship between self-esteem and confidence

We don't often think about the mutually dependent relationship between confidence and self-esteem, as we tend to view confidence as one of the *expressions* of self-esteem. We know high self-esteem drives high levels of confidence, and low self-esteem undermines confidence and drives compensation behaviours like defensive aggression and arrogance. We are aware that high self-esteem people own their mistakes without making excuses or falsely blaming others.

Confidence also plays a big role in building our self-esteem. It's one of those positively reinforcing virtuous circles that characterise the way human behaviour and mindset are conditioned into us. A confident person generates conditioning that continuously builds and maintains their self-esteem.

Courage

The third aspect of confidence is courage, in particular having the courage to push back appropriately with our family, our boss or our colleagues. How often do we come across people who aren't able to stand up for themselves, or who say, 'I'm not comfortable with conflict'?

'Conflict' is a revealing word: it primes us for negative outcomes. Yet not every situation in which someone has something to say that is corrective, seeks to change opinions or expresses a different point of view, is about conflict. People who see any interaction with another person that is not about agreement as conflict tend to avoid debate.

As a leader, you are likely to be aware that the people you value most are those who are brave enough to tell you what you need to be told. The absence of such courage damages organisations and leads to chief executive's disease: only being given information that's good or exciting. Obviously this distorts your view of what's going on and deprives you of the chance to be as effective a leader as you could be and contribute fully towards the organisation's goals. Leaders need members of their teams to have the confidence to tell them what's really happening. It's part of 'courageous accountability', one of my five characteristics of stand-out corporations (the others being extraordinary performers, positive leaders, emotional engagement and exceptional outcome ethos).

How to get zest

People with zest are positive, optimistic, motivated and emotionally stable with grit and resilience. They have courage, high self-esteem, faith in themselves, and consequently a lot of confidence. This winning mindset and the behaviours that arise from it have been shown time and again to deliver multiple positive outcomes.

How can we get zest? Quite simply by focusing on the inputs. Zest is not something we can feign in the hope that it will become real. We can't fake it till we make it. In this situation, we need to let go of the outcome – acquiring zest – and focus entirely on the inputs that deliver the outcome.

It's straightforward: if you want to have more zest, you need to make sure that the balance of your conditioning is positive. Ideally, arrange for everything that you experience in life – what you read, listen to, watch and your conversations with people – to be 75% positive.

I recognise that seems a tall order. As with many things that are well worth having, you'll require effort to achieve that balance. The good news is that my team's own research shows that people are better at this than at just about anything else to do with increasing zest. Every few years, we survey everyone who has ever passed through our programmes, and getting the balance of conditioning right always comes out top of the changes that people have made.

Zest is totally about positives in, positives out (PIPO). When you make sure that the vast majority of conditioning you allow into your brain is positive, your zest will grow and manifest itself in all aspects of your life. We will look at PIPO in more detail in Chapter 7.

THREE
Unconscious And Autonomic Game-changers

As human beings, we spend virtually all of our time in our conscious mind. It's how we experience being alive, so we attribute massive value to it. By contrast, we almost never get in touch with our unconscious mind. We don't know much about it, so we tend to undervalue it.

Freud has a lot to answer for: in his psychology, the subconscious (which to most people is synonymous with the unconscious) is the repository of dark desires and hidden causes of unhappiness. No wonder most modern psychologists talk about the unconscious rather than the subconscious, because we now know that Freud's model, in this respect at least, is not right.

The truth is that the unconscious mind is wholesome: it's our friend; it's our greatest mental asset; it's the source of all our good ideas and our solutions to complex problems – even though it may feel as though it's our conscious mind that is generating these thoughts. The unconscious mind has immense processing power and it never needs to rest. Once it begins to work on a problem, it does so continuously, drawing on a vast amount of information not available to the conscious mind. Think how often sleeping on a situation will present you with a solution in the morning.

The unconscious mind also has perfect self-knowledge – our entire self-concept (see Part II) – so it's far better than the conscious mind at making decisions about our preferred course of action when it comes to issues such as a promotion, a move overseas or an ethical conundrum. When we resort to the use of detailed lists of pros and cons, it's because we're trying to get our heads around a volume of information that is simply too big for our conscious mind to handle.

In this chapter, we'll be looking at some proven techniques for harnessing the power of the unconscious, giving you valuable tools for further improving your leadership and effectiveness.

Perception and reality

We've been brought up to believe, at least implicitly, that there is an absolute independent external reality that we should all accept. It turns out that that's simply not true. Reality is an individual subjective experience that we unconsciously construct for ourselves from our own personal perceptions.

Though I've used the word 'unconscious', 'autonomic' is sometimes a more accurate term, meaning hard-wired into the way our brain and nervous system operate. Our judgements and perceptions are skewed autonomically, so we are prone to making errors we're unaware of, unless we pay attention to this and compensate for it.

The truth is that human beings experience identical situations differently because their realties are different. Think of friends, family and colleagues who find situations you are totally comfortable with unnerving or even threatening. Eating a pistachio ice cream would be for some a delightful pastime, for others an unpleasant ordeal, and for yet others a potentially life-threatening nut allergy emergency. This is all governed by a process that you will know how to control from now on, drastically improving your experience of life, and thereby your outcomes.

Reframing

When I start teaching people how to exercise this control, I ask everyone to read through a simple sixteen-word sentence and count how many times they spot the letter 'f' in it – not because I want to check their reading skills, but to show that we'll get up to six different answers in the room. People sit there quite happily in their 3f reality among others who are in a 2f or 5f reality, but they are all quite certain that there is nothing wrong with the way they are seeing the world. But they can't all be right, can they?

There is a huge advantage in reality being made of perceptions (some of which do equate to the facts, obviously): it is that we can change our perceptions. And if we change our perceptions – the things our reality is made of – we obviously change our reality.

PARADIGM SHIFT FROM COMPANY-MAN TO ENTREPRENEUR

Many years ago, I was working with a newly promoted managing director of a leading utilities firm. Not long after I started working with him, he was fired after a fall-out with his boss. I continued to work with him as a coach and mentor and we quickly established his talents were better suited to running his own business. While he had often thought about it, he lacked the courage and conviction to effectively 'bet the farm' and go for it.

We became firm friends to this day and I'm proud to have played a role in unleashing his entrepreneurial talent. He co-founded what has become the world's leading provider of artificial intelligence to augment employee performance in the workplace and is a huge advocate of positive psychology. He even leverages the concepts in his technology.

In many circumstances, changing our perceptions comes quite naturally to us. Think about what happens when you're in a hurry and run into a solid traffic jam. Your initial reaction is likely to be frustration, anger or stress, but quite quickly you rationalise the situation, plan an alternative route or simply resign yourself to it.

At that point, your negative emotions subside so you become more comfortable. What you initially perceived as a disaster has become a mild annoyance that you can cope with – you have changed your reality. I call this process reframing and it's the simplest technique imaginable. Just ask yourself, 'How can I look at this differently and more positively?'

Pessimists are also expert reframers, but in the wrong direction. They need to be able to explain why things sometimes go well, so they use reframes like 'This is the exception that proves the rule' or 'Don't relax, it will go wrong again soon'.

What we are interested in is reframing uncomfortable situations in a way that allows us to rise above them more readily:

- Your flight's delayed for hours and the kids are acting up – but you're still going on holiday.

- Your house has been burgled and messed up – but you'd rather have your life than that of the unfortunate who did this.

- Someone you love dies – but focusing on how rewarding it was to have had them in your life rather than on your loss helps you to grieve healthily.

You can't change the fact that something bad has happened, but you can change how it makes you feel. And be in control of its impact on your CREAMS.

There is a simple truth about reframing: now that you know what it is, if you ever hold back from reframing an unpleasant situation, you are choosing to cling on to the discomfort you are experiencing. This is not a rational decision.

One brain, two systems

The human brain has two related but separate systems with which to think. These are a fast system (academic psychologists call this System 1) and a slow one

(System 2). I prefer to call them Hare and Tortoise to make it easier to keep their properties clear. Hare is intuitive, fast, automatic, effortless and involuntary. Tortoise requires effort, focus, is able to use logic and maths, and often involves choice and concentration. They're both essential systems with different jobs, and the interplay between the two is crucial.

Hare is constantly on the look-out for patterns and consistency – short cuts that enable us to process information quickly. It's why we tend to pay more attention to the content of a message or article than we do to its source – only when Tortoise kicks in do we evaluate credibility. Hare and Tortoise work together in this way to minimise cognitive effort by relying on Hare whenever possible. It's one example of a process called cognitive ease.

Expectations

How does the brain decide what it wants Hare to react to? It prioritises instantaneously through an autonomic system I call the attention algorithm. These are the signals that get priority:

- Strong signals: loud noises, sudden movements, flashing lights
- Threatening signals: mental or physical danger and risk

- Appetite-related signals: hunger, thirst, sexual attraction
- Expectation signals: things we expect to see

The main responsibility of the conscious mind is to keep us safe, including making sure we react appropriately to threats, opportunities to eat and drink, etc. Noticing potential mates is how we secure the future of the species and ensure that our genes are part of that.

The expectations element of our prioritising is perhaps counterintuitive. It dictates that we don't notice things we don't expect unless they are strong, threatening or appetite-related (STA) signals. This is a key concept in how the brain works, and the evidence for it has been demonstrated in a remarkable experiment.

GOING APE

In *The Invisible Gorilla*, Chabris and Simons described an experiment they had conducted.[13] Participants were asked to watch a video of basketball players passing a ball and count the number of passes made by one team. At the end of the video, they were asked whether they had seen the gorilla, which was in fact a girl in a gorilla suit, who crossed the screen, taking nine seconds to do so. Amazingly, only half of those asked had seen the gorilla.

---

13 C Chabris and D Simons, *The Invisible Gorilla: And other ways our intuitions deceive us* (Crown Publishing Group, 2010)

UNCONSCIOUS AND AUTONOMIC GAME-CHANGERS

> The effect was so strong that the people who missed the gorilla in the original experiment were completely unaware that they had missed something and didn't at first believe that they had. Astonishing – but the point is that we don't notice what we don't expect unless it's STA. As Nobel prize-winning psychologist Professor Daniel Kahneman puts it, 'We are blind to our blindness.'[14]

No doubt you can come up with parallels from your own life. Have you ever had to try to find your keys when you were in a hurry or stressed? Perhaps you gave up eventually and your partner had a go – only to find them in the first place you looked. Galling, isn't it? Clearly you must have looked straight at them first time round, but without seeing them. How could this happen?

The answer is that you'll have been thinking about your keys being lost, instilling in your mind a short-term expectation that they had disappeared. When your brain consulted the attention algorithm, it ran the usual check: STA? No. Expectation? The keys are lost. Your brain, therefore, had no reason to make you aware of it when your gaze fell on the keys.

The algorithm means that we will always notice the really significant threats, opportunities and signals. What about the things we don't expect, though? An

---

[14] D Kahneman, *Thinking, Fast and Slow* (Allen Lane, 2011)

optimist will notice all the things around them in the media that are consistent with their explanatory style – irrespective of whether they are signals or threats – because they expect positive events in the world. Conversely, if there is something negative in their environment, they will only notice it if it is STA. In their world view, such events are rarities, exceptions that prove the rule, because they simply don't expect them. Similarly, a pessimist will notice all the negatives, irrespective of STA, because they are expecting them, and miss all the positives except the STA ones.

This is where the availability heuristic comes into play: we tend to base decisions and opinions on events we remember, so inevitably we think such events are more frequent than ones we don't know about. After all, we don't know what we don't know, and this leads us to make the 'what you see is all there is' (WYSIATI) assumption, an acronym coined by Professor Kahneman. As a result, we undervalue what we are not aware of not knowing and are overconfident of the rightness of our perceptions and the decisions that we take on the basis of them. Even when information that contradicts our position is brought to our attention, we have an autonomic tendency to reject it for reasons of cognitive ease.

It's probably self-evident that the availability heuristic can lead us into making serious errors in business unless we guard against it. And what about the neutral things, which can be interpreted either way?

Optimists experience them as positives, pessimists as negatives because of Hare's autonomic assumption that there is a pattern based on our expectations.

Expectations of people

How do our expectations of people colour what we notice about them via the attention algorithm? We are largely unaware of our lack of objectivity about other people – in fact, we are blind to our blindness about them.

Think of a colleague whose work you admire. You know (ie perceive) them to be professional, capable and emotionally intelligent. Now use your awareness of how the algorithm works to ask yourself whether you will notice when they do something with professionalism or emotional resonance. The answer is yes, every time, no matter how trivial. If you're around when it happens, you'll spot it because you expect it. Not by choice, but by means of an autonomic process of Hare.

This explains two further phenomena:

- **The halo effect**, which dictates that if we like a person, we'll have an unfounded good opinion of everything about them, even attributing to them characteristics they may not possess that we value in people generally

- **Confirmation bias**, which makes us look for information that is consistent with our existing opinion, because as humans, we tend to look for patterns, and we seek cognitive ease as opposed to cognitive effort

The next question is whether you will notice when they do something unprofessional or emotionally discordant. The answer this time is more complex and can be surprising. If the deed in question is STA, then the algorithm tells us you will indeed notice it. If it is none of those things, then you will not become aware of the deed – furthermore, you will not even be aware that you have missed something. This is why we miss bad things that good people do, unless they emit the trigger signals. We are blind to our blindness.

Our good opinions of our colleagues are not always shared by those we lead. This means that when we miss an error by one of our stars, observers may well think we are just letting them off because of favouritism. That breeds resentment and damages our reputation as a leader. So beware: lack of objectivity is widespread and powerful, which is why we need to continually test our views of people against those of our trusted advisers.

By the same token, if we have a poor opinion of someone, we will be painfully aware of their every little slip-up because the events match our expectation of the person. On the other hand, we will not notice them getting things right because it's not what we expect, unless the relevant STA signals apply.

This has profound implications for redemption in the eyes of others. Once we have been labelled negatively in their minds, they will not notice our small successes, even when we turn our performance around. The algorithm is so powerful that they simply won't spot anything good that we do unless it's STA. Nor will they be aware that they've missed something. In fact, if someone draws their attention to our unremarked good deed, they will question it and may not be persuaded without evidence.

Neutral events are even trickier, as they tend to be interpreted in accordance with expectations. When a person who doesn't trust you becomes aware of a good deed of yours (because it's STA), they will assume you've done it for bad reasons and will probably come up with some unflattering explanation. This perception is their reality, and ironically is taken as further evidence in support of their erroneous opinion of you.

This is a huge issue for culture change. The legacy culture can set employees' negative expectations of leadership so firmly that they simply don't notice how far a leader's behaviour has changed, even in a new leadership team, but home in on every tiny lapse that conflicts with the new way. Furthermore, they will interpret much that is neutral negatively. This partly explains why I advise leaders not to expect people to hear their new messaging until they've repeated it five to seven times.

There is another fundamental message here. If our unconscious expectations are positive, the events and messages that we notice affect the balance of our conditioning positively. Our optimism, our relationships, our state and our CREAMS all benefit from this mechanism.

We'll cover how to change our unconscious expectations in Chapter 7: it's about conditioning, not willpower.

Action

Optimism, hopefulness and positivity always lead to better outcomes, but by themselves, they are not enough. We also need to take action. When doing so, we need to fix the widespread tendency to focus our emotions on the wrong thing.

Ask yourself this: when you're in the middle of a series of actions towards a goal, where do you invest your emotions? Most people focus on and derive their emotional reward – good or bad – from the outcome, which seems reasonable enough. After all, we're often told to 'start with the end in mind' and visualise the moment we achieve our goal. But take a step back and consider just what you are directly in control of from moment to moment. It certainly isn't the outcome. That depends on a number of factors that are outside your control, for example other people's actions and decisions, having the right strategy and so on. The only things you are truly in control of are the actions you choose to take.

Focusing on what you can't control can lead to learned helplessness, resulting in demotivation and giving up too soon. It's a classic situation with underperforming sales professionals worrying about prospects' decisions rather than their own activity levels. Their resulting negative state inhibits the very work rate they need to hit to turn things around. We all need to focus on the action, not the outcome.

Focusing on what we can control brings a sense of mastery over our results. We see this clearly in goal theory. Broadly speaking, we can divide our goals into:

- Outcome goals
- Performance goals
- Process goals

An outcome goal might be to win the club tennis championship. Towards that end, the process goal could be to practise for two hours every day, and the performance goal to bring full concentration and effort to every practice session and match.

In working with world-class sportsmen (the gender is intentional; sadly, I've only ever worked with males), I have always encouraged them to focus as much on performance and process goals as on the outcome. This avoids the danger that, as soon as it becomes clear they're not going to win a particular match, their outcome goal stops being a motivator and becomes something that crushes them. If their performance goals and, particularly, process goals are still in play, even if they don't win, they'll do as well as they can on the day.

The next thing to think about is when is the right time to stop? When we are pursuing a goal, we take action, and that action has a result. If the result is that we achieve our goal, we label that success and celebrate. If the result is that we do not achieve our goal, we label that failure and either give up, because we've accepted defeat, or try again. Eventually we reach the point where we conclude that either the goal is not worth further effort, or we are incapable of achieving it, and so we stop.

Getting the judgement right about when to stop and move on to a fresh goal has a big impact on our effectiveness and quality of life. It has become almost a cliché to say that success is born of many failures, that people who succeed have failed more often than those who do not succeed. The reason these sayings have become so hackneyed is because they are true.

Successful entrepreneurs understand that small failures are more precious than gold dust, whether it's the unsuccessful businesses they have tried as well as the ones they're famous for, like Lord Weinstock (who told a colleague of mine that he got about 50% of his acquisition decisions right, and that made him the best in the world), or the thousands of ineffective prototypes that littered the path to success of iconic engineering entrepreneurs like Edison and Dyson. Edison said, 'I have not failed, I've just found 10,000 ways that won't work.'

Look at the most successful sales professionals you know: they have the knack of drawing encouragement and inspiration from approaches that did not work. 'Every no brings me closer to the next yes' is another deep truth often labelled cliché by those who don't understand. Sometimes we give up too soon. It may be worth considering one final attempt from time to time.

Action, pessimism and optimism

I frequently meet people who want to be more optimistic. Most of them are already genuine optimists, but they're right – they could be even better at it. I never meet people who say they want to be more pessimistic. Even people who self-identify as pessimists at the beginning of one of my programmes are persuaded to pursue optimism once they have heard the overwhelming body of evidence about its benefits to effectiveness and quality of life.

Fear of failing is a good test of your optimism. Optimists are much better at dealing with disappointment than pessimists. This is because optimists spend more time in positive emotional states, and resilience is being built all the time they are experiencing positive emotions, so they are more resilient. Pessimists aren't less good at dealing with disappointment because of some character flaw; it's just that disappointment causes them more discomfort as a result of their lower resilience. All human beings are hardwired to avoid discomfort.

Pessimists expect success much less than optimists, so they have less reason to make an attempt, and this is compounded by the fact that failure is disappointing, the discomfort of which they are not good with. Fear of failure is sometimes a fear of disappointment. Optimists don't fear disappointment, so they are happy to make an attempt. This is partly why studies repeatedly show that optimists are more persistent, set more stretching goals and are better at getting them.

Failure sometimes gives rise to regret. The same resilience argument applies to regret as it does to disappointment. Nobody enjoys regret, and pessimists enjoy it even less because they find it more painful.

How powerfully you experience failure or regret might give you a clue as to the level of your optimism.

Learned ownership

In the context of positive leadership, ownership means taking responsibility without blame. It's the opposite of learned helplessness. This ownership is the responsibility that we choose to take for factors, tasks and events that others might not see as being part of our duty or sphere of influence.

When we pick up rubbish that somebody else has thrown on the street, we are not relieving others of their civic responsibilities; we're just owning the outcome that we want, ie litter-free streets. When we execute tasks that are part of an underperforming or overloaded colleague's job description, we're not excusing them from the duty to do a good job; we're owning the outcome that we want, ie good overall corporate performance.

Ownership goes with optimism. An optimist focuses on getting the outcome that they want; a pessimist focuses on the other person's failure and feels that it's not fair to themselves. The benefits of feeling in control of the outcomes that we want by owning them are enormous. Ownership delivers happiness, eliminates helplessness, gets noticed and brings success.

Sometimes it may be a question of reframing the situation creatively, but sometimes we need to take action. Suppose the person you share a home or office space with is in a foul mood. In this situation, you have two choices: to be helpless or to take ownership. Being helpless means you let their mood set the tenor of your day. Taking ownership means that you assume responsibility for how the day is going to go – in other words, you own their mood. It may not be fair that you have to make the effort to create a pleasant atmosphere, but who cares? You have the ability to get the harmony you want; you just have to do everything you can to alter their mood. What's more, your partner or colleague will really appreciate the selflessness of your behaviour, making it easier for the next essential act of ownership: empathetically holding them to account.

Adverse market conditions

Every recession results in corporate failures, but every recession also produces a few big winners. The classic response to a market downturn is to reduce costs, stop investing, consider downsizing and generally go defensive. For some businesses, this amounts to accepting reduced revenues and hoping to weather the storm. But this approach often results in long-term damage, so that even if a company survives, it is not well placed to take advantage of the resurgent market when it arrives. The perceived reality is that sometimes companies have to accept this fate – that's helplessness for you.

But what do the winners do? They take advantage of everyone else reducing activity levels and get busy. They recruit talent cut loose by the helpless, grab market share and invest. In short, they own the market conditions by taking responsibility for ensuring that their results don't take a hit. They see the market downturn as an opportunity and respond optimistically and courageously. It's tempting to think that this is only possible if your company is financially strong in the first place, but remember Richard Branson's strategy for dealing with a cash-flow crisis: expand.

Getting promoted

It's not my intention to give the impression that learned helplessness is an affliction of the weak and negative. Martin Seligman was the first to identify learned helplessness and his recent findings in this area are surprising.[15] It turns out that learned helplessness is the default state for humans, though we have a small specialised area of the brain whose job it is to counter it, so it's not really 'learned' at all. It's perfectly natural for a person to believe that whether they get promoted is in the hands of their bosses.

---

15 M Seligman, *Learned Optimism* (Knopf, 1991)

Those of us who have had a hand in promoting people know that isn't the case at all. Often the performance of a candidate means that it is impossible to do anything other than promote. Retaining talent is always in the mind of leaders, so if someone wants promotion, they can make the decision inevitable for their bosses by always doing exactly 100% of what is required.

That's how you take ownership of your own promotion. And taking ownership can also include having to deal with disappointment sometimes.

GIVING THEIR ALL

Shortly after Sir Clive Woodward returned to the UK having led England to triumph in the 2003 Rugby World Cup, I went to hear him speak about his Teamship approach. One less-than-positive individual in the audience challenged him aggressively during the questions, asserting that if Jonny Wilkinson had missed his spectacular drop goal, England would have lost, so all the talk of Teamship was beside the point. Sir Clive calmly answered that firstly England had a well-rehearsed last-minute strategy and he believed we would have scored in the remaining seconds anyway. He then added that if we had lost, it wouldn't have mattered.

The challenger was outraged, so Sir Clive explained that everybody in the team had spent the last six years doing exactly 100% of everything they could do to secure the

World Cup. If on the day they had met a better team, they would have been able to accept that. It would have been a disappointment, but no tragedy. He went on to say that had everyone only put in 98% and lost, they would all have felt gutted in the knowledge that they might have won had they just tried that bit harder.

This was a pure manifestation of ownership and of investing one's emotions in the action, not just the outcome.

It's clear that we can own every situation and every external influence through an appropriate combination of reframing and actions.

Priming

Finding out about priming for the first time is astonishing. If you give this process the respect it's due, it will change your relationship with words and thoughts.

Priming is the process whereby our decisions, actions, thoughts and emotions are programmed by a word we hear or see, or by another message in our environment, and is one of the hottest topics in psychological research. It's autonomic, so we are unaware of it and unable to control it. Amazingly, studies have shown that even if we do know it's happening, we are unable to resist its effect on us. This effect persists for a short time after the trigger.

The seminal experiment was conducted by Bargh at New York University.[16] Students were asked to make four-word sentences out of sets of five words. They were split into two groups. One of the two groups' words were laced with references to old age (without actually using the word 'old').

After the experiment, the students were asked to go to another classroom along the corridor for the next test. The whole purpose of the experiment was to measure how fast they walked along the corridor. There were several stunning results:

- The group with old age-related words walked significantly more slowly.
- None of the students noticed there was an elderly theme to their word sets.
- All were adamant they were not affected by the words they saw.

The point is that they never consciously thought of old age and its related slowness, but they were changed by the priming effect anyway. They were so unaware of its effect on them they took some convincing.

To emphasise the power of priming, bear in mind that this story has now primed both you as you read it, and me as I write it. Next time we move, it's going to

---

[16] A Bargh et al, Automaticity of social behavior. *Journal of Personality and Social Psychology*, 71 (1996), pp230–244

be slightly slower than it would have been otherwise. We won't notice and we can't prevent it; even if we run, it will be slower than it would have been.

Fortunately for our sense of conscious self-determination and choice (we like to feel Tortoise is in charge), the effects of priming are small – always there, but small. Experiments on priming voters have only changed the vote of a small percentage of people – mind you, that can be enough to reverse marginal results.

It's pretty obvious that priming has a massive impact on how we experience situations, what we make of them and our emotional reaction to them. There are some events our teams are sure to react well to, some they will find more challenging. Then there are events to which they might react either way. Those are the events where their behaviour is most likely to be changed by priming effects.

Give your conscious mind a go

Finally, it's only fair to let our conscious mind get a look in, despite the narrowness of its bandwidth compared to that of our unconscious mind. But this very narrowness is an advantage that we can use in certain situations.

We can exploit the fact that we can only handle one idea at a time if we really focus on that idea. When our minds are drifting, we can usually entertain more than one thought simultaneously – ironing while watching television and making a mental note to call a contact tomorrow – but as soon as we focus on one of them, everything else gets thrust out.

SEVEN IS THE MAGIC NUMBER

In 2005 a Dutch research psychologist called Dijksterhuis ran an experiment in which people were required to solve complex mathematical problems on a computer. Group A were just left alone to work their way through the problems. Group B were interrupted part of the way through each problem and told to count in sevens for ninety seconds. This meant that in Group B, each of the problems was delegated to the unconscious mind to solve while the conscious mind was occupied in counting. The result? Group B were 40% more accurate in their answers.[17]

I'm sure you're familiar with how difficult it is to stop thinking about distressing things at times. The harder you try, the more firmly the thoughts lodge in your brain, as anyone who has lain awake at night worrying will know. But if you want to throw an idea out of your mind, push another one in by focusing on it

---

[17] A Dijksterhuis, Think different: The merits of unconscious thought in preference development and decision making. *Journal of Personality and Social Psychology*, 87:5 (2004), pp586–598

with full concentration. Your conscious mind can only accommodate one of them.

By way of an illustration of how this works, suppose you are entering into a negotiation with a potential corporate partner, and you are feeling a bit vulnerable because your offering isn't complete. Your anxiety about this risks undermining your confidence in the negotiation, which is the last thing you want. But if you focus your thoughts on your goal, the doubts will literally be driven from your mind, leaving you free to deal with the situation confidently.

'It's all in your mind' is often used as a dismissive phrase, but this chapter has demonstrated how powerful and subtle a resource your unconscious mind is and how you can better deploy it for your own benefit as a leader, and for the benefit of your organisation and colleagues.

FOUR
Powerfully Influencing Followers, Stakeholders And Customers

In this chapter, we will cover the evidence-based approach I developed to enhance skills in influencing stakeholders, increasing sales and improving leadership and engagement. I call this approach Grace.

Just before the start of this century, Professor Daniel Goleman reignited researchers' interest in EI and its scope for enhancing human interactions. Since then our understanding of the benefits of applied EI in the workplace has been revolutionised. The research identified clusters of EI skills that deliver superior performance in a range of job roles and specialities. There are more than twenty of these emotional competencies, with six to eight usually being relevant to a particular role.[18]

Grace

After several years of using the excellent Emotional Competence model while working with leadership teams, I became increasingly frustrated that it was too complex for business executives to master and deploy in real time. We humans don't have the bandwidth to juggle twenty-three skill definitions while doing our day jobs, yet the need for such a real-time model was clear to me. I worked over three years to distil the research down to its key principles and hone the results, thus creating the Grace approach.

Grace is simple and quick to master, and it's based on the comprehensive research evidence showing that the key to influencing others is to focus on their emotional response to us. This applies whenever we seek to influence others as a leader, a follower, a sales professional or a team member, and when we seek to influence stakeholders in general.

In over twenty years as a corporate positive psychologist, I've not seen a faster, simpler route to powerful influencing than the Grace approach. It comprises four elements that form the acronym EROS:

---

[18] C Cherniss and D Goleman, *The Emotionally Intelligent Workplace* (Jossey-Bass, 2001); Goleman et al, *Primal Leadership*

- Empathy
- Resonance
- Optimism
- Self-esteem

Where those four essentials overlap is the super-powerful influencing zone.

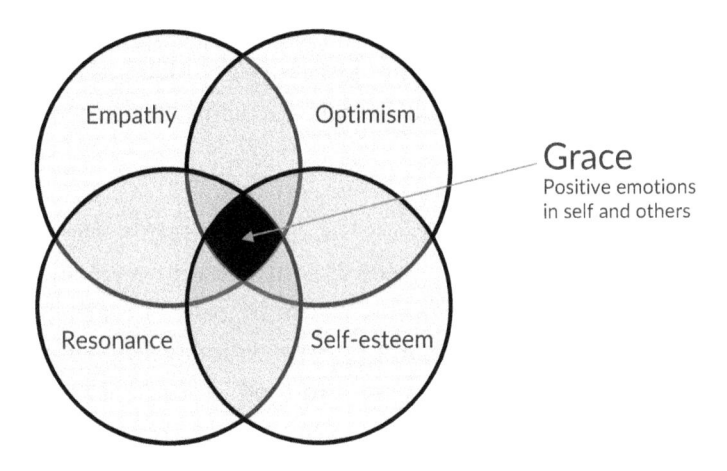

Grace
Positive emotions in self and others

Empathy

Empathy has three components, all essential in influencing others:

- Being able to see things from other people's point of view
- Sensing other people's emotions
- Caring about what they are feeling

As we saw in Chapter 1, our emotional connection with other people is strong when we are in a positive emotional state and collapses when we are in a negative state. Grace requires us to work on our own positivity and ensure that it becomes our default way of being. Losing empathy even momentarily can result in our doing or saying something that damages rapport, possibly for some time. We need our empathy to be fully engaged when we are trying to influence another person, otherwise we cannot tell whether we are resonating with them. Empathy is much easier to maintain if we are deliberately focusing on the other person.

Our empathy levels depend on our genetic inheritance and our learned behaviours as well as on our own emotional state. Some people are simply more empathetic than others, and maintaining an emotional connection to other people feels natural to them. Indeed, I came across one senior executive who was such a natural empath, we had to develop strategies to protect him from being overwhelmed by other people's emotions.

Leaders who wish (or need) to improve their empathy will be pleased to know that it is a learnable skill.

Resonance

In our present context, 'resonance' is a term from the psychology of EI. It means impacting others' emotions positively: always generating positive states in them and never triggering negative ones. When we are consciously centring our attention on someone else's emotional state, it is much more likely that we will resonate with them – this may be obvious, but in practical terms it's frequently not easy to achieve.

Resonance is the kernel – the indispensable essence and absolute purpose of Grace. Without resonance, it is impossible to achieve your potential for influencing other people. The whole point of Grace is to help people achieve resonance and avoid its opposite, dissonance.

If, for example, you make a person feel disrespected, patronised or bored because you're going too slowly, or confused because you're going too quickly, their attention is on dealing with the negative emotions you've triggered: 'I wish this person would hurry up and get on with it' or 'What are they on about?' They are not focused on your message; they are waiting for you to stop talking so that they can deal with their frustration.

When you trigger positive emotions, for example, when you make people feel respected, liked, valued, interested, excited and engaged, they think about what you are saying rather than how you make them feel. They may have a background awareness that their engagement with you is a pleasant experience, but above all, they will focus on the information you are presenting. They will then respond to your influencing efforts on the basis of the merit of your point of view as they see it, and that is the best you can ethically do. In other words, resonance earns us an opportunity to be judged on the merits of our arguments.

Optimism

Goleman and others' work clearly identifies optimism as one of the essential characteristics of leadership excellence. We know that optimism means expecting positive outcomes and entails interpreting your environment through a hopeful and constructive explanatory style. People find optimism attractive in leaders and influencers, and are disinclined to give their discretionary effort to pessimists.

When they are optimistic, leaders bring people with them. On the other hand, not even pessimists like to be led by other pessimists. But it is also true that having a level of optimism the other person sees as excessive inhibits rapport. It's important to keep our focus on others to ensure we are resonating with them, so that we know when to adjust.

Self-esteem vs arrogance

As I explained in Chapter 1, self-esteem is a wholesome self-regard and sense of self-worth. It's included in the Grace influencing model for two reasons:

- In any interaction, it's vital to take care of the self-esteem of the other person, otherwise resonance between the participants will be lost because of the negative emotions triggered.

- Successful influencing is all about focusing completely on the other person, and it's hard to maintain our focus on others unless we feel fundamentally content with ourselves.

If we have low self-esteem, we naturally prioritise meeting our own needs, and don't necessarily notice the effect we have on those around us. Equally, unless we care for the self-esteem of the other person in an interaction, we can't be certain that we are resonating with them. Low self-esteem gives rise to behaviours like saying something because of our need to say it, not because of the other person's need to hear it, or failing to take ownership of the need to fix the situation when something we say gets taken the wrong way.

There is a misunderstanding that arrogance arises from an excess of self-esteem. In fact, arrogance is the result of poor self-esteem; it's a compensation behaviour. Those who genuinely have a lot of self-esteem recognise when others think they are being arrogant and change their behaviour accordingly to put people at ease again. In the same situation, those with low self-esteem ramp up the arrogance, thinking about their own importance and feeling the need to convince other people of it.

Resonance and behavioural style preferences

If you listen to a badly-tuned talk radio station, it can be impossible to hear what people are saying – the signal – because of all the hissing and crackling – what engineers call noise. Similarly, there's an awful lot of behavioural noise between human beings that can hide or swamp the signal, caused by our misinterpreting unconscious behavioural traits as having meaning.

One key purpose of the many behavioural style metrics available is to separate the noise from the signal in another person's behaviour. When noise overpowers signal, resonance can be lost and dissonance can take hold.

Consider the four types drawn from my Style-Lyte metric. Each style is named after its strength and the weakness that appears when that strength is taken to excess:

- **Dominant/domineering (D).** Dominant people take action, provide direction and naturally take the lead in a group. In excess, they become domineering, close others down, are offhand and won't listen.

- **Measured/mean (M).** Measured people are all about logic, working things out carefully, precision and completeness of data. In excess, they fail to share data, become slow and are oblivious of deadlines.

- **Giving/gullible (G).** The giving person is selfless and supportive. They support because they have a need to do so. In excess, they give support when others don't want it, and fall prey to inappropriate guilt.
- **Warm/weak (W).** The warm person is affable, flexible, loving and kind. In excess, they put other people's interests ahead of their own and can appear weak because they seem to do whatever anyone wants.

If a person never shows the excess behaviours associated with their style, as is commonly the case, it doesn't mean they've got the wrong style in mind. It's because they are on top of their vulnerabilities.

People of different styles frequently misinterpret one another's behaviour as containing information (signal) when in fact it's just about behavioural preference (noise). A dominant person might get frustrated with a measured person, deeming them too slow, pedantic, overcautious, even obstructive. A measured person can in turn find a dominant bossy, reckless and impatient. Warms are often thought to be lightweights or frivolous, and givers fussy and interfering. In point of fact, none of that is true; it's all just a manifestation of how each style naturally behaves.

When a dominant asks you to go quicker, it's not that they're being impatient, just that they like pace. When a measured wants more data, it's not because they're being overcautious, just that they see a material risk. Warms need harmony and fun, but that doesn't mean they don't see serious issues and give them due weight.

What we need to understand is that we interpret others' behaviour on the basis of what that behaviour would mean if someone of our own style was displaying it. When a warm seeks more data, there's real meaning in it – but not when a measured does so. When a dominant makes a joke, they are probably expressing dominance rather than seeking harmony. When a giver starts to take control and get stern, they really are hacked off, whereas with a dominant it means nothing, it's just their style.

Circumventing all this potential confusion is deceptively simple. When it comes to real-time interaction, it really isn't necessary to work out other people's style according to your company's metric of preference. You don't need to remember how that style relates to yours and what you're supposed to do about it. In constructing a team or assessing a team member's role compatibilities, it's good to exploit the information such metrics give you, but if you're just seeking resonance on the hoof, whether it's with someone you know or a stranger, there's an effective short cut.

In establishing resonance, the trick is to assess just three elements of a person's style preference. With practice, it's easy to do this in real time and it soon becomes automatic. Then all you have to do is flex your behaviour to bridge any gap between their style and your own.

The three behavioural style factors to focus on and adjust are pace, detail and task:

1. Pace: does this person like to work fast, or do they like to take things more slowly?
2. Detail: does this person want comprehensive information or just the conclusion? Do they prefer to work things through or trust a gut reaction?
3. Task: is this somebody who is focused primarily on task or the people elements?

Getting pace, detail and task right not only builds resonance, but avoids the dissonance that can arise when we confuse signal and noise.

Scale of impact available through Grace

Studies to examine the impact of resonance on sales effectiveness continue to show that there are significant material benefits.[19] Compared to their peers of

---

19 Cherniss and Goleman, *The Emotionally Intelligent Workplace*, p50

similar experience, sales professionals who excel in Grace-related skills achieve 123% more sales in conquest business.[20] Even more strikingly, studies have shown that in account sales, resonance delivers additional sales performance of between 400% and 567%, depending on sector.[21]

IMPROVED SALES AND REDUCED SICKNESS ABSENCE

Jill was an engineer and serial entrepreneur who had recently sold her telecoms company to a global major on a 100% earn-out asset-sale basis. The company had three major issues: poor sales performance, high levels of discretionary sickness absence and low morale. The impact on revenue and profits was so severe that Jill was looking at a pay-out that would not even fully repay the borrowing she had taken out to support the business before the sale.

I quickly diagnosed what was driving the negativity and helplessness that were behind the company's problems. These stemmed from the psychological reaction to a period of tough trading conditions culminating in a rescue sale to a former competitor. I designed an intervention to boost positivity, end helplessness, re-engage management and staff, and increase motivation – with the ultimate objective of transforming EI and

---
[20] Sloan and Spencer, Participant survey results
[21] C Cherniss and D Goleman, *Competency Study Database* (Hay/McBer, 1997)

> Grace. Over a period of six months, we rolled out the three-day programme to the extended leadership team and all customer-facing staff: sales professionals and service engineers totalling just under 30% of the head count.
>
> Sales doubled and sickness absence reduced by more than 90%. Eighteen months later, Jill received her final earn-out payment, which was enough for her to repay her creditors and retire in the sun.

In one of my favourite pieces of research, Professor Richard Boyatzis of Case Western Reserve University looked at the relationship between resonance and CEOs' profitability records. He assessed individuals' skillsets and looked for any relationship between them and the financial results of the business unit they led. All of the businesses in the study were units within one of the global consultancies (not named in the study).

It turns out that the key CEO's skill cluster in delivering profit is a combination of diligence and Grace, which gives rise to a 390% improvement on peer average EBITDA. Interestingly, Professor Boyatzis found that the improvements conferred by above-tipping-point relationship management skills were a mere 110%.[22]

---

22 RE Boyatzis, Developing Emotional Intelligence [unpublished paper] (Case Western Reserve University, Department of Organizational Behavior, 1999), quoted in Cherniss and Goleman, *The Emotionally Intelligent Workplace*, p39

> **REFLECTIONS ON GRACE**
>
> Spend half an hour tonight thinking about the Grace skills of your key team members, using EROS. Predict where they might be losing resonance with their own teams and identify opportunities for them to improve one of the EROS elements to win more complete followership.

The power of Grace is awesome. In a world where psychologists and consultants love to invent complexity, I am inspired by such a pure, simple concept:

- If you want me to follow you, then make me feel valued, inspired, safe, special – not criticised, less important than you, threatened or embarrassed.

- If you want to sell me something, boost my self-worth, show me you're interested in my needs not yours, respect my decision process instead of telling me what I should think, value my time, don't bore or frustrate me, and give me the level of detail I need, not what you prefer.

- If you want to relate well as my fellow team member, let me know you care about my outcomes. Trust me, value my affectionate respect. Don't make me feel less than you, a rival, manipulated or irrelevant.

Grace is all about resonance. But we can't expect to resonate just like that; we need to build our awareness and manage our behaviour in relation to all four elements of EROS. Grace is also a word with many meanings. It is about unconditional love, gratitude, selflessness, being blessed, economy of action, generosity of spirit, elegance and…

…*power.*

PART TWO
CHANGING OURSELVES

In the late twentieth century, something remarkable happened in science. Two breakthroughs were made in separate scientific disciplines that drew the same conclusion and transformed how we think about behavioural change. The development of cognitive behavioural psychology in the 1980s was followed in the mid-1990s by an explosion in our understanding of the brain. This gave rise to the branch of neurobiology called neuroplasticity. Both explain how behavioural change occurs in human beings and how to take advantage of these mechanisms.

FIVE
Cast-iron Personal Change

We have all likely been brought up to believe that it is through strength of character and force of will that humans can change how they think and, much more importantly, how they behave. It turns out that is not right.

There are a couple of phenomena that have allowed our Victorian view of human change to persist. One is that, every now and then, we try to change by exercising our willpower and it appears to work. Because we seem to have achieved what we wanted to achieve, we think it should always work. In fact, it is an unconscious process called cognitive-behavioural conditioning that delivers change – but precisely because it happens in our unconscious, we are not aware of it.

The second phenomenon is neuroplastic change: the synaptic and chemical changes that happen at the intracellular level in the brain (which we will explore in the next chapter). Again, we have no real-time awareness of it. That is why both of these processes fool us into thinking that willpower works.

We are also fooled by some exceptional people who demonstrate the most incredible feats of willpower – and become renowned for doing so. We end up thinking that everyone, ourselves included, ought to be able to demonstrate that level of willpower. Take my friend, who was the chief executive of a major insurer and is currently a much sought-after non-exec director and chairman. He has run ultra-marathons through the Sahara, trekked to both Poles, scaled Mount Everest at the age of sixty and rowed the Atlantic in his sixty-seventh year. Such people are famous precisely because they are so incredibly rare.

When most of us try to bring about change through willpower and fail, we draw negative conclusions about ourselves. If only we were like the people we read about in the newspapers! We think we're not strong enough, that we're doomed to failure and that there is something wrong with us. This destroys our self-esteem, and as we saw in Chapters 1 and 2, the behaviours that self-esteem engenders are vitally important.

Why willpower always fails

The reason that willpower fails us is that the conscious part of our mind has a bandwidth of about 300 bits per second, which compares, for instance, to a domestic broadband bandwidth of, currently, between 10 million and 100 million bits per second. This means that our conscious mind is only capable of focusing on one thing at a time, and our brain is hardwired to ensure that one thing is the job of keeping us safe. The brain detests it when we use our conscious mind for something else, like suppressing our habitual behaviour, and puts a stop to it as soon as it can.

It is part of our unconscious mind, termed the self-concept, that controls our behaviour from second to second. This is the part of our psychology that drives our default behaviour and mindset. Human beings have default settings just as computers do, and the techniques in this book are about changing these default settings.

There is little added value in terms of commercial performance in teaching business people how to reach super-peak performance at one point in time. In sports psychology, we need people to be at that utter peak for a few seconds or a few hours; in business, though, we are interested in adding massive value by transforming people's routine, ie default performance levels.

How does willpower fail us as leaders in a work context? Imagine a challenging situation – maybe a conversation with a report who is being slow on the uptake or slightly obstructive, isn't giving their full co-operation and is frustrating us. Most people in that position will reach a point where they become exasperated. Unless we exert self-control at that point, our behaviour – what we do naturally – changes. We lose emotional connection with the other person and become impatient, critical, maybe even discourteous.

As a leader, we've then lost resonance, lost the report's followership and damaged the relationship. We know intuitively that this is not what we want, so we override our undesirable natural reaction by suppressing it through the exercise of willpower in our conscious mind. We are now using the strength of our will to stop ourselves doing what comes naturally to us. The conscious mind has taken control of our behaviour and the brain will not allow that to happen for any longer than it absolutely has to, because when we are controlling our behaviour with our conscious mind, that takes up all of its bandwidth, leaving nothing to fulfil its number-one job, which is to keep us safe.

The brain identifies this as a dangerous situation. At the first opportunity or distraction, maybe when stress levels reach a tipping point, the brain will return control of our behaviour to our unconscious mind. At that point, our natural behaviour comes out and our irascibility, frustration or dissonance are no longer suppressed.

We tend to call this – incorrectly – reverting to type. All that has happened is that our willpower has failed, as it's supposed to. That's because willpower is there purely as a short-term emergency intervention for when we need to do something that goes against our deeper instincts.

That's why willpower will always fail. It's designed to. It never evolved as a way of bringing about permanent changes in our mindset and behaviour. Indeed, current research is examining whether willpower is a finite resource that gets depleted until we allow time for it to replenish. The theory is that if we engage our willpower towards one end – for example, managing the impact of our stress levels on our anxiety – we will have less or even none of it left over to apply to other purposes, such as remaining resonant with a recalcitrant report. One thing is certain: permanent change in our mindset and behaviour happens only through cognitive behavioural conditioning and neuroplastic change.

The self-concept and conditioning

The source of how we think, feel and behave is a psychological construct called the self-concept. Everything there is to know about a human being lies in their self-concept. Think of it as our master-program. It governs how we behave with people that we care about, how we behave with people that we're indifferent to and what we do in any given situation; it shapes our leadership style and habits, our project and time-management skills; it determines how good we are at the piano or our chosen sport, and how well we sing. It dictates whether we are meticulous about diet and exercise to maintain a body weight close to the one we want, or whether we're constantly yielding to the temptation to eat the wrong things, have too much alcohol and not exercise well enough. All this is embodied in, and expressed from, our self-concept.

This results in an apparently uncomfortable truth, which is that everyone, in terms of how they think and behave, is exactly who they believe themselves to be. We are who we know ourselves to be because what we are doing is continuously expressing our self-concept. This is an autonomic process. We can't, in the long term, behave in a way that is inconsistent with our self-concept. If we try to do that, it gives rise to stress.

A classic scenario in corporate cultures is that someone who reaches a high level of seniority then has some sort of breakdown and becomes dysfunctional. As I moved up through the management ranks in the accountancy profession, many of my friends reached a point where they couldn't take the stress any more – not because they were weak, but because they were actually being too strong, overriding their self-concept to deliver a level of hard work and commitment that was not natural to them. In fact, stress is a disease of the strong. But overriding the self-concept in the long term is unhealthy, and not everyone is able to do it.

If you have the self-concept of somebody, for instance, who overeats and under-exercises, then that will manifest in your behaviour patterns, and you'll end up having a body size and shape that you're probably not comfortable with. It's not easy to accept that you look like this because this is who you know yourself to be, deep down in your self-concept – especially when you want to change so much and have tried so hard, but have not yet succeeded.

The good news is that by changing our self-concept, we can all make the behaviours that will create our ideal version of ourselves become our default behaviours. By doing so, we inevitably achieve our goal.

Conditioning and cognitive behavioural change

The message of cognitive behavioural change is positive because it says, for example, 'Your attempt to change how you look through willpower is always going to fail. What you need to do is to change your self-concept, and when you acquire the self-concept of somebody who exercises and eats well, that will automatically start to generate healthy diet and exercise habits, which will deliver the body condition/size/shape that you aspire to.' So we need to learn how to change our self-concept.

The self-concept is created and updated by conditioning. Conditioning is a process of unconscious learning that happens to every human being continuously. Every second of every day, we are learning about ourselves from everything that we experience. For example, the messages that our parents gave us when we were tiny, telling us that we are good looking, clever, capable, kind, impressive, or naughty or lazy, constitute powerful conditioning that shapes our self-concept.

If you tell a child that they're hard-working, they will become more hard-working. If you tell a child that they are naughty, they will absolutely deliver on that for you. In the corporate world, when you tell one of your reports that they are more capable than they realise, this conditioning gets into their self-concept. Eventually, with repetition and reinforcement through their own self-talk, this will manifest in improvements in their effectiveness as they automatically deliver on that change to their self-concept. The reason this doesn't always work is that no amount of encouragement and praise by a boss can overcome the opposing impact of a person's internal negative self-talk.

If you are in a corporate culture where people love and praise the organisation, and are full of affectionate respect for its leadership, this ethos forms the backdrop of the informal conversations that go on between people throughout the organisation, and those attitudes and behaviours are conditioned into everybody's self-concept. This is one of the ways that cultures take hold, and it manifests in a workforce and extended leadership team that are highly engaged.

If, on the other hand, you are in an organisation in which people are super-critical in a negative way – where any success, however remarkable, is always qualified by saying, 'Yes, but what happens next?' or 'Yes, but we could have done even better' – the opposite culture develops, as everyone's self-concept takes on harmful norms. When it is fashionable to be cynical about the business or the market or the leadership team, that is the conditioning people in the organisation are subject to. If it starts being cool to be negative, or to be a smiling cynic, then cynical, disengaged cultures arise. More pragmatically, this is often how the potential for positive cultures and aspirational levels of engagement in organisations gets undermined.

The key to bringing about changes in our mindset and behaviour is for us to actively manage all of our conditioning. We need to change our conditioning environment so that the lessons we are unconsciously learning from it move us to where we want to be. All too often, many elements of the conditioning content of our environment are counterproductive.

It's helpful to think of our conditioning environment as comprising four areas, all of which we need to actively manage to achieve the best results:

- People
- Media
- Environment
- Self

In the people category, we find colleagues, bosses, reports, family and friends. Media include newspapers, advertising, social media, the internet, literature, film, television, radio, podcasts and so on. Environment covers factors such as race, gender, religion, political affiliation and socio-economic group. Some of these are obviously not amenable to change, but how we think and talk about them definitely is. Which leads us to the self: the most pervasive and continuous source of conditioning, comprising everything we think, say, remember and do. As a rule of thumb, we want the sum total of the output of these four elements to be 75% positive, as well as directionally correct.

Positives in, positives out

There is a Freudian misunderstanding about conditioning that we need to deal with. This is that the older a piece of conditioning is and the earlier it happens in our life, the more powerful it is. There is a widespread

CAST-IRON PERSONAL CHANGE

belief and, indeed, good anecdotal evidence to suggest that childhood experiences are formative.

More recent cognitive behavioural psychology tells us that the reason childhood experiences have a strong impact on certain individuals is not only because of the power of the experience itself, but because the individual has been reliving that experience ever since. It is the way that we tell ourselves the story of our childhood experiences that imprints the impact of those experiences into our current psychology. We remember things hundreds or thousands more times than they actually happened. The impact is in the remembering.

Research into traumatic childhood experiences has shown the massive therapeutic benefit of taking a cognitive restructuring approach with those children in later life, helping them to change the way they think about the traumatic experiences. It turns out that it is the last three or four times they retell the story to themselves that actually determine its impact on their current psychology.

This is a general phenomenon: it is the most recent conditioning a human being experiences that has the biggest impact on their mindset and behaviour. It's impossible to overestimate the significance of this in the context of achieving change by mastering our conditioning.

Choosing happiness

In 1995, the father of positive psychology Martin Seligman was in the garden with his five-year-old daughter, Nicky. She said to him, 'Daddy? Remember last year I had to stop whining? And that was the most difficult thing I ever had to do. If I can stop whining, can you please stop being such a grouch?' Nicky was clearly a precocious child, to be able to make such a statement at the age of five, but that's maybe not so surprising given that she is the daughter of arguably the world's most famous psychology professor.

Her comment brought him up short and he realised that she was right. At that point in his career, Seligman was one of the world authorities on depression; he resolved to become an equal authority on happiness and that's how positive psychology started.

In 2003, after years of research into happiness by an increasingly wide community of professionals, Seligman decided to change the psychology profession by training 1,000 psychologists in positive psychology – I was in the first class. By this time, the change in him personally was astonishing. He was happy, smiley, confident and looked more like the chief executive of a FTSE 100 company than an academic.

Seligman provides a perfect demonstration that if we change our conditioning from depression to happiness, we change our default state from grumpy to jolly.

We can all do this by taking control of our conditioning rather than passively consuming everything that happenstance throws into our lives. In other words, we can manage our own conditioning. Many people do this naturally, but the key is to become meticulous about it.

Most leaders want to set a better example. They want to be emotionally stable, so that they are always calm and measured in their leadership interactions. They want to achieve more of their personal potential to become even more successful. And they want to win the engaged followership of the people they're responsible for leading. They need to demonstrate some specific behaviours, such as diligence, resonance and courageously holding people to account in a constructive way (more on these in Chapter 7). They also need to become even more positive, so that they achieve high-performance defaults via CREAMS.

We can avoid dooming ourselves to failure because we're relying on willpower by taking active control of our conditioning environment so that it becomes 75% positive. Most people's conditioning is 70%–90% negative, so I'm talking about a 180-degree shift. In corporate leaders, the balance will almost certainly be more positive than that, as evidenced by their success, but unless we are at 75% positive, there is still room for improvement. We have the potential to shift our explanatory style in the direction of high performance, to become even more positive and optimistic as a person while still remaining grounded and keeping our judgement fully operational.

For over twenty years, I have been encouraging senior executives to eliminate every bit of negative conditioning they *reasonably* and *responsibly* can from their environment. I can't help but admire the discipline and focus I see in people as they reduce their exposure to negative social groups, cherished but negative TV programmes and excessive consumption of new media. The result is that they default to positive emotional states, experiencing negative emotions much less often. They reap the full benefits of CREAMS: maximising creativity, EI, analytical reasoning, motivation and self-esteem in the moment, and strengthening their resilience and self-esteem over time. Likewise, their Grace and influencing skills grow as their focus shifts more towards other people, improving both their empathy and resonance. Leadership skills reach new levels, followers flock to them, engagement soars, and the resulting additional efforts accumulate bigger numbers on the bottom line.

To be directionally correct, we must ensure our behaviour-specific conditioning spawns and reinforces aspirational behaviours, actively moving us towards the version of ourselves that we want to be. For example, we can talk into existence the high-performing, charismatic version of ourselves that we aspire to. On the other hand, we need to be careful not to speak our weaknesses and fears into existence.

In the wider context of our conditioning, in the areas of media and people in particular, we don't want to expose ourselves to conditioning that undermines our behavioural commitment to being a great leader, hitting the gym regularly, valuing and respecting people, having a rich and fulfilling home life, and so on.

At every moment of the day, we are making tacit choices about our conditioning environment, and now it behoves us to become more active in those choices. We need to intensify our awareness that if we take control of our conditioning, we will move our self-concept in the direction that we want. And when our self-concept changes, then our default mindset and behaviour also change. This is automatic, always succeeds and cannot be defeated.

In the next chapter, we'll look at the extraordinary science of neuroplasticity and the brain's immense capacity to change and adapt. Understanding how to develop new pathways in the brain has the power to revolutionise our success as leaders.

SIX
Resetting Your Brain's Defaults

Imagine the beauty, subtlety and awesome power of the structure that brings you the consciousness through which you are perceiving these words. It's daunting even to begin.

The consensus estimate is that the brain contains 100 billion neurons (brain cells)[23] which communicate with one other via a network of 500 trillion connections. To make the connections, each neuron has branching tentacle-like structures called neurites, of which there are two types:

- Dendrites to receive information. Each neuron has a large number of dendrites, which are fewer than

---

[23] H Green et al, Molecular neurobiology and genetics: Investigation of neural function and dysfunction. *Neuron, 20:3* (1998), pp427–444

2 mm long – ten times the diameter of the cell body (soma).

- Axons to send information. Each neuron usually has only one axon, which can be up to a metre long – huge by comparison (if the soma were the size of a football, the axon would be up to three-quarters of a mile long).

Neurites connect to other neurons where an axon from one neuron meets a dendrite from another; that junction is called a synapse. What goes on in synapses is complex, profound and still not fully understood. Remembering Einstein's view that 'everything should be made as simple as possible, but no simpler', for the purposes of our model, we will say that neurons connect via neurites.

Neurons can be in contact with up to 500,000 others and operate like sophisticated routing exchanges. They receive information as electrical impulses, identify and process it, compute which route to forward it along, and then despatch it accordingly. The processing power this constant activity requires exceeds that of any computer in existence (at least until quantum computing becomes a reality).

Clearly there are some tasks at which our PC outclasses us – arithmetic, for one – but in most other respects, there is no competition. For example, the continuous visual processing each of us unconsciously performs

RESETTING YOUR BRAIN'S DEFAULTS

would require a bank of 1,000 supercomputers to duplicate.

If each neuron can be in communication with up to 500,000 of its fellows at a time, then how many different possible 'sets' of its neighbours can each individual neuron connect to? In other words, in how many ways can a neuron be configured? If you are like me, you will need to pause to take in the answer:

10,000,000,000,000,000,000,000,000,000

Impossible to visualise, isn't it? Ten thousand trillion trillion. One followed by twenty-eight zeros. Mathematicians write this as 10^{28}.

Compare this to the possible configurations of each processing unit in a computer: two (hence 'binary'). The building blocks of our brain are more complex than their computer equivalent by twenty-seven orders of magnitude. Imagine the difference in capability this represents. That's a big idea to take on board, and the best is yet to come.

If each individual neuron can be configured in 10^{28} ways, and we have around 100 billion of them, how many configurations is the brain capable of, taken as a whole? The figure is too big to write in this book – it would take an astonishing *three million* volumes like this to contain the figure. It is estimated that the handwritten number would be a line of figures 10.5 million kilometres long. That would stretch from here to the moon and back forty times.

With numbers that big, it's easy to accept that our brains, as many researchers believe, have enough storage capacity to remember the details of everything we experience in our lives. We retain everything, although we cannot consciously recall it all at will.

In passing, it's worth exploding one or two myths. First, it has long been thought that brain cells don't have the ability to replace themselves like other cells do. It has now been found that neurons, in fact, do have some capacity to regenerate themselves. Furthermore, the so-called 'no-go' gene responsible for inhibiting neuron regeneration has recently been identified. If science can discover how to disable the gene, serious neurological disease and injury may well become reversible.

Second, we have likely all heard that our brain cells are gradually dying off, particularly in later life. What is less widely appreciated is that the rate of cell loss is completely insignificant compared to the huge numbers of cells we have. To illustrate the point clearly, the average weight of an adult male human brain reduces by *only 1%* over a lifetime – an insignificant reduction in mass, which, given what we now know about the unused potential of our brains, can be more than compensated for by regular mental exercise.

The brain is in some ways like a muscle – it needs exercise to get fit and stay that way. When we exercise regularly and appropriately, we build our muscles. By exercising our brains appropriately, we can build our mental strength and increase our intellectual capacities. Provided we can avoid brain disease, we can retain mental capability as we age by using our brain (and there is some evidence that using our brain fully reduces the risk of Alzheimer's). Our intellectual capacity is driven not by the number of cells in our brain – that is broadly the same for the vast majority of people – but by the number of connections between them. Mental exercise builds connections.

Make your brain think, make it work, give it exercise. You will be repaid a thousand-fold.

Forging pathways in our brains

The relatively new science of neuroplasticity discovered that thought is a flow of electrical energy from neurons along neurites to other neurons. This energy can be tracked and measured – indeed, you may remember the impressive infra-red photomicrographs published in the *Sunday Times* in 1998, showing the physical path of a thought traced by the sequential firing of groups of neurons. What then became clear is that a particular thought is associated with a particular group of neurons and the pathway linking them.

A particular thought always uses the same neurite pathway. When we have a new thought, we create a new physical pathway in the brain, and whenever we have that same thought subsequently, it uses that same neurite. Our thoughts change the physical structure of our brains – continuously. Were we able to compare what the inside of our brains looks like from one year to the next, we would be able to see the neurite structure changing.

There is immense power in this insight. *We can rewire ourselves at will with the power of thought alone.* This is no flimsy theory of self-improvement. This is scientifically established fact.

We can visualise a line of thought, or the thought process which accompanies a particular sequence of actions, as a chain of neurons linked by neurites – physical links between real physical objects. Each neuron represents a point at which the path of our thoughts, and therefore our actions, can diverge in one way or another. How does our brain decide which way to go at any point, which of the alternatives to choose?

Electricity, like water, always follows the path of least resistance. In the physical world, thoughts are electrical impulses flowing between neurons, as we have seen. Stronger neurite pathways have lower resistance than weaker ones. Our thoughts will follow the path of least resistance like any other form of electricity – that is, the one of the strongest neurite pathways.

What makes one neurite stronger than another? The answer is use: neurites grow and shrink according to how much use they get. Every time our thoughts travel along a neurite, it grows slightly stronger; if left unused, it weakens. So every time a neurite is used, the chances of it being used again increase slightly. Every successive time we have a thought, it gets easier to experience it again. Repetition breeds repetition.

Establishing a new line of thought is not unlike making a new footpath through the jungle with a machete. The first time we establish the line of the footpath, it's hard and slow because there are lots of branches to cut away. The next time it's easier because the trail is already blazed, particularly if the jungle hasn't had long to grow back. The third time, the path is getting wider and it's easier still. From then on, the process takes progressively less effort each time, until we take the new broad path for granted.

We have all had experiences of mastering a new skill, such as learning to drive a car. For a lot of us, it was a little bewildering to begin with: getting things in the right order, co-ordinating the steering, gears, clutch, handbrake and so on. After a couple of lessons, we began to get the hang of it, and eventually became skilful. A few months of regular driving, and the whole process became automatic. The neurites were well established, strengthened by repetition, and the actions we needed to take at any point lay down the path of least resistance.

The fact that our thoughts follow the most used neurites is great news for people whose habitual thoughts are empowering, happy, confident, dynamic and positive. It is less good for those who are in the habit of having thoughts that lack self-belief, are full of fear, undermine confidence, are lethargic or bring on sadness. Positive people are more likely to keep having positive thoughts because the positive neurites are the strongest. Similarly, negative-thinking people are likely to stay that way – unless they intervene to change things.

The practical upshot of this is that habits of thinking are self-perpetuating, and the joy is that we can see how to eliminate negative patterns of thought and replace them with positive ones. We can use this phenomenon to bring into being new self-perpetuating patterns of thought – and thus of action – that will transform our lives.

Let's take a common example: diet. Most of us at some point become concerned with managing what we eat for one reason or another. Whether we are trying to reach or maintain a target weight, follow a healthier diet or be true to our ethical convictions, we all have to learn to overcome the temptation of the forbidden chip, chocolate bar, bacon sandwich or whatever our personal dietary Achilles heel happens to be.

Imagine you are confronted with your Achilles heel on a plate – all you have to do is pick it up and start eating, but your present goal is to cut that item out of your diet. You are at a decision point: there are two (at least) alternative neurite paths your thoughts can follow:

- Path A might go something like this: 'Oh boy, that looks gorgeous – just one bite won't hurt. Mmmm, that's so good – maybe one more bite. Yummeee – oh blow it, in for a penny, in for a pound. That was *good* – but now I feel awful. Why can't I resist?'

- Path B could go more like this: 'That does look good, but think of what it would do to me – and I really don't need it. Funny how I'm less and less tempted nowadays – perhaps I'll have an apple instead. Well done, me, I'm proud of myself!'

Which path will you go down? Obviously the stronger neurite, the one you habitually follow. If you usually weaken, you probably will again. If you always give in, you certainly will do so this time as well. If you normally resist about half the time, you've a fifty-fifty chance of doing so this time. It's all a question of the relative sizes of the neurite paths.

Increasing the chances of going down the paths of our goals, rather than the paths of our usual behaviour, which we want to change, is simply a question of building up the positive neurites and allowing the negative ones to atrophy. Guaranteeing that we *always* travel down the path of our goals merely requires us to make sure our goal neurites are strong and our old behaviour neurites are shrivelled and weak. When we achieve that, goal-realising behaviour is automatic – the laws of physics and our physiology make absolutely certain of it. If we know how to enlarge one set of neurites and shrink another, all we have to do is travel down the goal neurites repeatedly, and never again travel down the negative ones. Simple.

But if it's so simple, why do so many of us fail at it so much of the time? The answer is that most of us try to stick to our goal neurites using willpower alone to resist our habits. As we now know, we will always slip back into the old ways using this method because it's an attempt to force behaviour that conflicts with our self-concept, which is not sustainable in the long term. We are compelled by our psychological hardwiring to act in concert with our self-concept.

Fortunately, we can take advantage of other properties of the brain to build our goal neurites without the need to overcome any willpower challenges at all. And it works every time.

Mental rehearsal

I BELIEVE I CAN FLY

I'd like you to join me in a simple thought experiment if you would.

If you want to get the most out of this section, stop reading when I say, 'Now' and close the book until you have five minutes when you are alone and unobserved to give the experiment your full attention. Continue only when you are comfortable, relaxed and unconcerned by the possibility of interruption. Then pick up the book again and start again from where I say, 'Welcome back.'

Now.

Welcome back. Please get comfortable in your chair or bed, but stay sitting reasonably upright and follow these instructions:

- Close your eyes and make an effort to steady your breathing.
- Consciously relax your shoulders.
- Empty your mind as well as you can. Gently but firmly push away any thoughts that come into your mind.
- Take three long, deep breaths in and out. Repeat until you feel relaxed, then open your eyes and read on.

Visualise this situation:

You are standing on a high promontory, looking down into the valley below. There is no guard rail, but you feel secure for the moment. The wind is blowing through your hair, sometimes gusting quite strongly, rising in strength all the time. The sound of it grows in your ears and its power forces you to take a step back.

You hear the crunch of gravel underfoot and realise that your footing is not secure, that you are standing on a steep slope of loose stones. You stumble and the wind catches you, whipping away your sunglasses. The sudden bright light blinds you and you feel increasingly disoriented, conscious of the precipice close at hand, but you are not sure exactly where.

The wind is howling now, plucking at your clothing, lifting you off your feet. You stretch out your arms to regain your balance and the wind seems to exult at the additional hold this gives it on your body. The lifting force is growing inexorably, and incredibly you start to rise into the air. Your toes lose contact with the ground for a moment, then again, this time for longer.

Then a particularly strong gust whisks you into the air. Suddenly you are yards away from safety, seemingly suspended over the yawning gap below. You are flying – and for some mystifying reason, you feel absolutely safe, totally secure in the knowledge that this is a dream, you are in no danger. You are not surprised when the wind returns you to earth, then quickly fades away entirely.

RESETTING YOUR BRAIN'S DEFAULTS

You are on safe footing. The adventure is over. You walk away smiling and feeling better for the whole experience.

Take a couple of breaths again and reflect on the experiment.

What did you experience? You may have felt apprehension or anxiety, particularly if you are uncomfortable with heights. If you aren't, you probably felt rising excitement, the brief exhilaration of flight, perhaps followed by disappointment when the game ended. What I'm sure of is that, if you co-operated with the experiment, you will have felt something, and you will have noticed changes in your body. Increased heart rate, heart in mouth, a smile or a grimace, maybe even gripping the arms of your chair more tightly. Many people experience even stronger physical reactions.

Let's examine some other examples – no more practical experiments, though, so relax!

Have you or has anyone you know ever manifested physical symptoms of fear during a movie? Perhaps it was a long time ago, but do you remember covering your face with your hands, hiding behind the settee, leaving the room, jumping out of your seat or even screaming just a little? Physical reactions all.

I clearly remember the first time I experienced ceiling-to-floor 180-degree surround-screen cinema at the National Air and Space Museum in Washington DC in 1986. I will never forget the sight of 200 people, standing on a completely stationary concrete floor, suddenly nearly falling over and grasping frantically for the handrail as the picture on the screen, filmed from the cockpit of an F15 fighter, banked hard to the right and went into an afterburner climb. Wow! Most of us have had a similar experience even at ordinary cinemas: physical responses to sounds and moving images.

At another level, most of us know people who have phobias. Have you noticed that even the idea of the phobia object or situation, sometimes a picture or model of it, can trigger the fear response? I'm not trying to make light of what can be a debilitating clinical condition, merely highlighting the lessons we can draw from it.

Have you ever blushed when recalling embarrassing events in your past? Has your heart ever skipped a beat when you're thinking of your new-found love? Have you ever shivered when thinking of what might have happened, for example, if you hadn't checked on your children when you did, only to find them playing dangerously? Have you ever become excited when thinking of a past or an imagined passionate encounter? Have you ever cringed at a gruesome passage in a novel?

Our reactions to all of these situations have one thing in common: we are reacting in the physical world to events which are occurring only in the mental world. It happens all the time. Thoughts and memories can produce physical reactions in us, sometimes with enormous power. The explanation of this common phenomenon is as follows:

The brain cannot distinguish between real and imagined events.

We can use this characteristic of the brain to build new positive neurites without recourse to superhuman doomed-to-failure efforts of willpower. If the brain cannot distinguish imagining or thinking about an event from the event itself, then isn't it reasonable that every time we visualise that event, we are reinforcing the neurite structure that relates to it? This is indeed what happens, and it's one of the most liberating facets of this whole area of endeavour. Whether we are doing a thing or imagining doing it (mental rehearsal), the identical neurites are firing in our brains. And when they fire, they strengthen. Mental rehearsal can create new dominant pathways that embody the thinking or behaviour we are targeting.

It literally means that we can fatten up our positive neurites by visualising the achievement of the goal to which they relate. By incorporating such mental rehearsal exercises into our daily self-development routine, we can grow the goal neurites we want and let the others wither.

How to use mental rehearsal

Every time we mentally rehearse the new behaviour we want to achieve, the neurites relating to it enlarge slightly, and the chances of our naturally manifesting it increase. With lack of use, the neurite relating to the old negative behaviour we are replacing begins to shrink. After a time – maybe just a few weeks (since new neurites take about six weeks to form strongly) – we reach a point where the old and new neurites are of equal size.

This is a critical moment. All we need to do is travel down the new neurite once more – by mental rehearsal or actually manifesting the new behaviour – and it becomes stronger than the old. The battle is won from that point on, and we will find we no longer need to think about adopting or visualising the new behaviour. Our thoughts, and thus our actions, are following the path of least resistance, ie the stronger neurite. That is now the new behaviour neurite, the goal neurite.

In other words, our goal has become our natural behaviour. Usually we are unaware that this has happened until some time later, when we suddenly realise we have not shown the old behaviour for a while and we have stopped thinking about it. The first time this happens – and it will – the sudden realisation of what is actually going to be possible is like a jolt of positive energy and excitement.

The effectiveness of mental rehearsal and visualisation has been exploited by international sportspeople for decades. Professional golfers visualise every single shot in competition and the perfect swing in practice, mentally travelling down this neurite path time after time, reinforcing their golf shot habit. Olympic bobsleigh teams have very little time to practise on a run, and they need to have the whole course imprinted in their mind – tiny variations in line make the difference between winning and being out of the medals table. They spend hours in mental rehearsal, visualising the ideal run, building the neurite pathways that will take them along the perfect winning line.

THE PERFECT ROUND

The most stunning story of all is that of US Colonel Naismith, who was a Vietnamese prisoner of war for seven years, confined in a space so tiny that he could hardly move around. He knew that to survive the ordeal, he needed to find a way to keep his mind occupied, so he began to spend hours every day in visualising playing golf.

Every day for seven years, he visualised the perfect round, constructing as much detail as he could, taking just as long as he would in reality. In his mind's eye, he nailed every drive, hit every green and sank every putt. When he was released and had got fit again, this heroic man played his first round of real golf in more than seven years. He had been a high handicapper the last time he had played, typically going round in 90+ strokes, but now he scored par or 72 – a transformation in standard resulting purely from the new neurite pathways he had built in seven years of mental rehearsal.

The *Sports Psychologist* reported a study of a diver developing a dive for the Olympics that had never previously been performed successfully.[24] He spent a year trying to visualise pulling that dive off, without success; he couldn't even see it going right in his mind's eye. Then he got the hang of it and visualised it for another year, now seeing it working well. Not until after those two years of mental rehearsal did he actually physically practise the dive in the pool. For his third and final year of preparation, he combined mental rehearsal and physical practice. Then he took gold with his dive at the Olympics.

Mental rehearsal physically builds new neurite pathways. I've seen this first-hand in my work with Tour pro golfers, an Indy Car-winning racing driver, and thousands of entrepreneurs and corporate leaders.

---

[24] T Orlick and J Partington, Mental links to excellence. *The Sports Psychologist*, 2 (1998), pp105–130

Emotion accelerates change

There is even more we can do to accelerate the process of building new neurites. Emotion has a potent impact on the rate at which neurites grow.

Imagine a curious toddler trying to get to the oven while her parents are busy cooking in the kitchen. Every time she moves towards it, her mother or father gently blocks the way and says, 'No, darling – don't touch that – it'll burn.' But curiosity is a powerful driver and the urge to explore is strong. The toddler keeps trying, the parents patiently and firmly keep repeating the same message. They may have to repeat it scores of times over the weeks before the toddler gets the message and accepts that the oven is not to be touched. The new neurite has become established.

Now imagine what happens if things go differently. After the first dozen foiled attempts, the child takes advantage of both parents' attention being elsewhere for a few moments and makes it to the oven. With a little laugh of triumph, she plants both palms firmly against the oven door. Big ouch! Tears and commotion ensue, her parents half distraught at her distress, half cross with themselves, each other and her.

Will they ever need to repeat the warning? Of course not: the child has well and truly learned the lesson. A new 'hot ovens burn' neurite has instantly come into being, already large and strong enough to make sure that it is always the thought path of least resistance for the rest of the toddler's life. Where scores of low-key warnings had failed, a single intensely emotional event succeeded.

This is an example of an important general rule:

Intense emotion builds big neurites quickly.

The reason is that emotion floods the brain with high levels of the neurotransmitters that are essential in the formation of new neurite pathways. It's then easier to build stronger pathways faster, and this can cause acceleration by several orders of magnitude – from a few weeks to a few microseconds, as with our imaginary toddler.

We can capitalise on this – the more emotion we put into our mental rehearsal and visualisation, the faster it will take effect. Intensity and frequency of repetition both help to build new neurites, and intensity is *by far* the more powerful.

In the next chapter, we'll look at the techniques we can exploit to capitalise on the plasticity of our brains.

SEVEN
Programmable Self-programming Humans

It's no exaggeration to say that we are all the product of everything we've ever said or thought to ourselves. These thoughts and words are how we condition ourselves, and they have consequences for our behaviour as leaders and the way we communicate with the people we want to be our followers. Our effectiveness as leaders depends on our conditioning ourselves in the right way.

We've already established that willpower is not enough for bringing about change. Only conditioning brings about change, and we are in control of our own conditioning.

Self-talk

Self-talk is an immense resource for conditioning ourselves into becoming the version of ourselves that we aspire to, rather than just allowing ourselves to be randomly programmed this way and that by our surroundings without thinking about where this might be taking us. Self-talk is:

- What we say about ourselves
- What we say about the world
- What we think

The concept of self-talk was first introduced in the 1970s by the American child psychologist Shad Helmstetter in his book *What to Say When You Talk to Yourself*.[25] Since then, his approach has gained acceptance in the world of research psychology and positive self-talk is recognised as a fundamental technique to master to achieve our potential. It is an essential part of sports psychology, performance psychology and organisational psychology.

It's happening continuously, whether we're aware of it or not: we're constantly programming our future selves. It's up to us to intervene positively in that endless flow.

---

25 S Helmstetter, *What to Say When You Talk to Yourself* (Harper Collins, 1986)

When I teach people about self-talk, I spend fifteen minutes defining and illustrating how it works. At the end of this time, I ask the class, 'What is the purpose of language?'

They invariably answer, 'Communication', and nothing further, even though I've just demonstrated that the purpose of language is also conditioning. This goes to show the degree of paradigm shift that we need to make to take charge of language for our conditioning.

A NOTE ON NATURE VERSUS NURTURE

While I know we are all capable of change, I'm not claiming that we can change ourselves into a different kind of person. People talk about the concept of nature versus nurture in this context as if it's an ongoing debate, but this issue was resolved long ago.

Our genetic make-up sets a range in which we are capable of performing for every human attribute and skill. Where we actually end up on that spectrum depends on conditioning – on our self-talk. The difference between somebody achieving their full potential and achieving little of their potential is the difference between them being assigned to special needs education and being capable of getting into a top university, and it can be down to the type of conditioning they have received about how to use their brains, as noted by Frederick Goodwin, formerly the director of the US National Institute of Mental Health.[26]

Not to take advantage of how the mechanism of conditioning works is to risk leaving your potential unfulfilled.

Our pesky Pleistocene brains, unfortunately, mean that a lot of our self-talk is critical and destructive. Unless we manage it carefully, it will push us in the wrong direction. Once we intervene to replace this negative self-talk with positive talk, we can generate a virtuous circle in which our self-talk creates and updates our self-concept, which drives the behaviour that we default to. This then becomes more positive, which in turn generates more positive self-talk, and so on – the process becomes faster and faster.

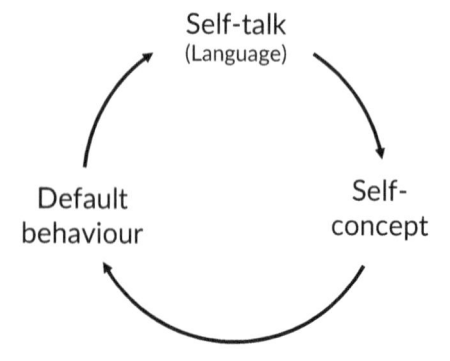

Self-talk
(Language)

Default behaviour

Self-concept

We also need to take into account, as well as the content of our self-talk:

---

26 R Kotulak, *Inside the Brain* (Andrews McMeel Publishing, 1996), p4

- Tone of voice
- Body language
- Behaviour

The same three words spoken in a different tone of voice can be a compliment, an insult or a joke. Our posture and gestures can completely change what we are saying, too. If we're shaking our fist at somebody and hissing through gritted teeth, 'Just think before you open your mouth', we're meting out a terrifying admonishment; the same words delivered calmly with a squeeze of the hand are a gentle piece of advice from a friend or parent.

This effect is no less powerful when directed at ourselves. Think of the extent of negative conditioning that takes place when you sneer at yourself in the mirror for some misstep that you've magnified out of all proportion. It's far better to put on a smile and say something positive to yourself about the day to come.

When we know how destructive behaviour can distress others, why would we turn it on ourselves? The furious reactions we sometimes see in tennis players, smashing their rackets to the ground and grimacing, are not the best conditioning for calmly playing a devastating return at the next serve.

To give an example of how our behaviour can influence our self-concept more widely, suppose you were to hear a conversation that you disapproved of because it was racist or sexist or malicious in some other way. Calling the speakers out for this is a positive behaviour that will nevertheless generate some trepidation, as you want to handle the situation well and can't predict how they will react. The strong emotion you will experience will ensure that this trepidation as part of a positive behaviour is reinforced for the next occasion, showing just how dynamic a process conditioning is.

Self-talk traps

Sometimes we're aware of how unhelpful our inner monologue is; often, though, we just don't recognise that the things we are saying, to ourselves and to others, may be having the opposite impact from the one we intend.

The first trap that we fall into is that we forget we are self-priming all the time (I described the priming mechanism in Chapter 3). Imagine that you have to conduct a termination interview with a senior colleague that you respect and care for. Clearly, it's going to be an extremely uncomfortable experience.

When your PA comes in to announce that he has arrived and asks you sympathetically, 'Are you OK?', you may say something like, 'This has to be one of the most difficult things I've ever had to do. I hate this part of my job.' You have just primed yourself to be ill at ease in the forthcoming interview, and this has conditioned you to be even more uncomfortable in similar situations in the future. Although the interview is a situation in which you need to be operating with your mental and emotional faculties working at their best, your negative priming means that your CREAMS are impaired and you become less capable than you were.

How should you answer? You still need to acknowledge your PA's kindness and concern, but follow it up with something like 'Nobody loves this situation, but I know I'll handle it well.' Now you have primed yourself for confidence and empathy.

Snake words

There are dozens of words that we use every day that do more damage than we give them credit for, operating as negative triggers. The word 'hate' is a case in point. People use it in a way that closes their minds to any positive possibilities, and it becomes what I call an 'incantation', because the power of this type of negative self-talk is almost magical. It often leads to a bout of venting, in which a whole succession of negative events and connotations is evoked. Not surprisingly, it has a powerful conditioning impact.

One of the worst misunderstandings of popular psychology is the received wisdom that venting helps to get things off our chest. It doesn't – getting things off our chest just forces them more deeply into our self-concept. We may experience momentary relief when we go off on one, but in fact we'll just have conditioned the negative emotion even more deeply into ourselves, which means we'll need to do it again.

We could say that this 'offloading' is in fact 'onloading', because we can find ourselves caught in a venting loop. To break this vicious circle, we talk about the solution rather than the problem. Instead of dwelling on the pain we're experiencing, we describe the relief that we wish to experience.

'Struggle' has become a fashionable word, perhaps because it's a kinaesthetic word, evoking physical movement. If you are describing something to yourself as a struggle, you are automatically making it more difficult for yourself, because the word's use will impair your CREAMS.

Imagine a situation where your boss comes in and asks about the project you're leading. If you answer, 'Well, we're struggling, I'm afraid', you've just primed yourself into negative thinking, and thereby taken the edge off your ability to get it done.

The table below gives just a few examples of snake words, and the alternatives you can use to avoid them. No doubt you'll be able to come up with plenty more.

Snake words and how to avoid them

Replace:	With:
Hate	Dislike
Struggle	Adventure, challenge
But	And
Problem	Challenge, solution, opportunity
Difficult	Not easy

The useful thing about negative words and prefixes is that the brain doesn't notice them. This means that when you substitute 'not easy' for 'difficult', you are still describing accurately how hard the task is, but it's the word 'easy' that your brain picks up on, with the result that you have just primed yourself positively for the next time you think about that task (more on this in a few paragraphs).

Throwaway comments

Throwaway comments may seem like light, insubstantial utterances, but they have the potential to take us away from where we want to get to as a person.

Suppose someone says to a colleague, 'I'm going out for a walk at lunchtime to get some fresh air. Do you want to come?' and they reply, 'I can't be arsed.' What the colleague is actually saying is, 'I lack the motivation to do something that I would enjoy and I know is good for me.' Yes, they're telling the truth – most self-talk that is damaging is also true – but they've primed themselves in the short term not to do something positive, and have entrenched in their self-concept the belief that they lack motivation.

Throwaway comments relating to emotional states only exacerbate those states: saying 'I'm nervous' or 'I'm exhausted' will do nothing to calm a person down or liven them up. In the second example, instead of connecting with their energy, they've connected with their fatigue.

Correcting self-talk

Our negative self-criticism about the faults we see in ourselves may arise from a wish to fix these faults, but it just makes us worse. If we tell ourselves we're stupid five times a week, we don't become a stupid person, but we do damage our self-esteem. The way to overcome this self-talk trap is to find a positive way of saying something negative – correcting self-talk, in effect.

We need to use positive self-talk all of the time so that it becomes a default response. In extreme circumstances, such as an accident or a traumatic family event, we won't have the bandwidth to remember that this is one of the occasions when we have to use positive self-talk to prime ourselves to handle the situation effectively. But if we've conditioned positive self-talk to be a habit, it will be there for us when we really need it.

We can even develop a self-talk script: a string of positive sentences that tell our story the way we would like it to be, addressing ourselves in the second person and using our own name. In a 2014 study, Professor Ethan Kross found that the '…subtle linguistic shift – shifting from 'I' to your own name – can have really powerful self-regulatory effects.'[27]

Recording a self-talk script can be helpful, not least because we don't even have to be listening to it consciously for it to work. Just having it on in the background will have a positive conditioning effect.

Meet the white rabbits

'White rabbits' is my shorthand for a phenomenon you may well be familiar with. If someone says, 'Don't think of a white rabbit', the image of a white rabbit will be the first thing that pops into your head. The brain ignores negations.

The negativity bias of our Pleistocene brain, combined with our brain's inability to conceive of an absence, means that much of what we may think of as supportive self-talk is the exact opposite. As in the example

---

[27] E Kross et al, Self-Talk as a regulatory mechanism, *Journal of Personality and Social Psychology*, 106:2 (2014), pp304–324

related to 'difficult' above, if we say to ourselves encouragingly, 'I'm not scared', the brain ignores the negation and all that's left is 'SCARED!'

It's worth noting that this applies beyond self-talk, too. If you're calling everybody for a meeting in the morning and you tell them 'Don't be late', you're in fact priming them all for lateness. This will have no impact on most of them, but it might just tip someone who is on the edge over into behaviour that makes them late.

There are many harmful white rabbits that we deploy every day when talking to ourselves and to others. I'm sure you'll recognise some of these:

- Don't be late
- Don't forget
- It's not all doom and gloom
- Don't mess this up

If you're calling a meeting because there's something that needs a quick solution, trying to reassure everyone by saying 'It's not all doom and gloom' will just mean that they'll be spotting precisely that in everything you say. They'll have lost their edge because you've put them in a negative state. Likewise, anyone to whom you say 'Don't mess this up' is being primed for disaster.

Far better to speak positively, ie prime them for what you want to happen:

- Be on time
- Remember
- There's good news
- Make a good job of this

We can exploit the brain's property of ignoring negations to craft helpful white rabbits, for example substituting 'not easy' for 'difficult', 'not comfortable' for 'nervous' and so on. Our meaning is clear, while the priming effect is created by the positive word – just what we want.

In fact, there's *always* a positive way of saying something negative. My best effort is surely the occasion when I had a puncture, lost control of the car and ended up in a field late at night. I rang home to say, 'Sorry I'm not going to be back as early as I intended, but three of my tyres are fine, and the trees look interesting from this side.' As well as priming myself for being resourceful (it was late at night, I needed to be), this avoided the anxiety and alarm I would have caused by saying, 'OMG, I'm stuck in a field, I've had a puncture. What on earth am I going to do?'

In these situations, we don't have the presence of mind (ie the bandwidth) to carefully phrase things in the right way. Our default patterns of speech come out automatically. If we want to manifest positive priming and helpful self-talk in extremis, we need to practise it as our norm, all day, every day, no exceptions.

HOW ARE YOU?

A stark example of how positive priming matters is the unthinking answer we tend to give to the casual query, 'How are you?' In one way or another, we generally answer this question dozens of times a day – that's dozens of opportunities to condition ourselves.

People who answer 'Fine' are conditioning themselves to be just that. There's a link between their usually feeling no better than fine and the years of conditioning themselves dozens of times a day to feel that way. They say fine because they feel fine. They feel fine because they say fine. Their self-talk loop is in a mediocrity cycle in this regard.

My advice is to upgrade your stock response, making sure to resonate with the people around you, from good to great or wonderful. Sometimes 'awesome' is OK, sometimes even 'excellent' might dissonate. My personal favourite was inspired by Zig Ziglar: 'If it got any better it'd be against the law'. Perhaps I can get away with that because of my job!

Make it true

It's important to note when you're correcting your self-talk that lies don't work. There is a world of difference between finding a positive way of saying a negative thing and the kind of baseless bluster that people who are insecure deep down resort to. You can be perfectly truthful about your abilities or your faults by using helpful white rabbits like 'I don't find forecasting as easy as I'd like to' or 'It takes all my patience to go through the data'.

Now we have the keys to making positive changes to the way we think and feel, in the next part of the book, we'll look at how leaders can harness the power of this approach to create a winning ethos.

PART THREE

THE WINNING ETHOS

We've proven the case for both the benefits of positivity and human beings' overwhelming capacity to change. What remains is to consider how to manifest a company's full potential for profit, growth and employee wellbeing in synergy: the winning ethos.

EIGHT
Resonant Leadership Mindset

I often ask people, 'Who makes you a leader?' The answer, of course, is followers, though it's not the answer I always get.

We can decide to be a leader, we can achieve a senior role responsible for hundreds or thousands of people, but until someone says 'I will follow you', we are not leaders, just people with authority. This means that it's possible for some people to become leaders even though they don't necessarily want to lead, just because other people follow them.

What is it about resonant leaders that makes people follow them? The answer is simple: if you trigger positive emotions in others, if you make them feel respected and confident, safe and inspired, they will give you the opportunity to be heard on merit and commit their followership to you. This is not at all the same as just being kind; that doesn't begin to constitute resonant leadership, not least because if you're simply kind, you don't, for example, give people enough developmental feedback or confront others on their behalf when you need to.

Conversely, despite the fact it's wrong and a seriously outmoded view, I *still* encounter senior managers who have the impression that to be a leader, they have to be a hardass. They micromanage, boss people around, even reprimanding their reports in front of others and attempt to motivate with threats. I call it weakness masquerading as strength, and unfortunately people who have been managed or led in this way often reproduce it. Even the kindest person can be quite scary to their reports and teams if they are sufficiently senior.

If this is you, the solution is to ramp up your empathy and resonance. Be on guard against being perceived as autocratic, especially if there was a history of that before you arrived on the scene.

Resonant leadership, or leading with Grace, is about doing our own job to high standards, always triggering positive emotions in others (particularly when holding them to account), never flinching from courageous accountability, and displaying genuine warmth and optimism. Others respond with their followership and taking our leadership initiatives to heart. Highly effective leadership is as simple as that.

How can you tell whether you are being resonant with people, or whether you are, however inadvertently, generating negative emotions in them? It's helpful every now and then in a leadership interaction to check on how you are being received by asking your follower. Don't expect them to be completely open with you, but ask them anyway. Signalling your genuine desire to understand, adding positive feedback and encouragement, builds and sustains empathy.

EROS is my tool for leaders to undergo a 360-degree assessment of their resonance. Even in good people, the results often show profound disparity between how they see their empathy, optimism and resonance, and the degree to which others perceive these qualities in them. In these cases, they need to start with taking the focus off themselves and their own needs, and putting it on to other people and their needs.

Leading with Grace

Leading with Grace entails having the mental toughness and the emotional resilience to do what needs to be done on behalf of the greater good, even if it's not pleasant. Your team needs you to be strong and prepared to go in to bat for them when necessary, whether it's tackling someone who's not aligned with the organisation's agenda and not pulling their weight, or fighting for the resources needed to fulfil the business strategy.

A PRE-EMPTIVE STRIKE

One of my clients was a divisional CEO who won a big promotion and found himself in charge of 7,000 people. He did what most people do on being newly appointed to a senior role: he took a step back, looked at what was happening in the markets and realised that his industry was heading for a major recession. As a result, he made 1,200 of his workforce redundant. It was a testing exercise to go through, but he was vindicated. There was a massive recession and similar companies went under, but his survived; he had saved the majority of his employees by acting decisively when he did.

This man is one of the most resonant leaders I know and genuinely more focused on other people than himself. There could be no better demonstration of this than the roadshow he set up when the redundancies were announced. He arranged to meet those he'd made redundant in groups and came clean, saying, 'Nobody told me to do this. It was my decision. It's for the greater good. What do you want to say to me?'

That strength of character and emotional resilience exemplifies the highest standard of leading with Grace.

Top traits of resonant leadership

Resonant leaders share some notable attributes…

- High self-esteem, so, among other things, they are not preoccupied with their own image/status/weaknesses etc

- Genuine empathy with others: the ability to sense the emotions of another person, see things from their point of view and care about it

- Resilient positivity: maintaining an even emotional keel even when things are going wrong, rather than becoming thoughtless or irascible

- Ability to trigger positive emotions in their followers, even when they are giving corrective feedback, by criticising the behaviour rather than the individual, and ensuring the individual understands that the intention is to bring out the best in them

- Sincerity – people can sense when leaders are merely feigning warmth and affection for them, and one of the fastest ways of losing followership is being a phony

...and ways of behaving. They:

- Know when to direct, mentor, coach, consult or give free rein. Their focus on others enables them to identify the best approach with their reports.

- Hold others – and themselves – to account courageously. They can be relied on to do the right thing, even though it may mean challenging someone senior or addressing an uncomfortable truth.

- Are able to exercise tough love. Their followers can trust them both to give the necessary development feedback and to take the far from easy decisions.

The high levels of engagement that result from resonant leadership yield significant benefits. Teams are happy and energised in their workplace and put in considerable discretionary effort (see Chapter 9). In such high-performing teams, people and results grow in parallel. It's a virtuous circle in which individuals are drawing on their maximum potential so teams are doing well, and it shows in increased revenues and profits. The chatter on social media becomes increasingly positive, making it easier to attract and retain talent. In turn, superior financial results inspire individuals and teams and add incremental value for the ownership of the organisation.

For the resonant leader, the rewards include the followership of their teams and even their peers, and respect from bosses, shareholders and other stakeholders, all of which open up new career possibilities and opportunities.

Dissonant leadership – and the consequences

You may recall from Chapter 2 that zest is the word I use to describe both high-performance mindset in individuals and business cultures that deliver superior revenues, profits and growth. Zest comprises positivity, hope, optimism, drive, energy, motivation, resilience and persistence. To have a zest culture, an organisation needs a near-universal zest mindset throughout the people that comprise it – just a few key influencers who go beyond responsible enquiry into pessimistic dissidence can undermine it.

Taking prompt decisive action with cultural dissidents is essential to limit the damage they otherwise cause, both to the timely achievement of corporate goals and to top leadership's credibility if destructive dissidence is tolerated. To aid in identifying how to proceed you can sort the people in an organisation broadly into four categories:

Category	Description
Champions (high-impact positive people)	Usually the leadership of the organisation – their personal agenda and that of the organisation are perfectly aligned
Supporters (low-impact positive people)	The people who actually get the work done
Dissidents (high-impact negative people)	Destructively champion an agenda in conflict with company goals and ethos (different from minority opinions that appropriately seek change – an obvious strength)
Downbeats (low-impact negative people)	They block and question everything, resist change and put in the minimum amount of effort – as destructive as their high-impact counterparts

It's essential to work on your dissidents, giving them the opportunity to embrace zest and an appropriate length of time to master it. You need to adopt a cognitive behavioural approach, as with any behavioural and thinking change.

When dissidents turn into champions, instead of holding you back by 10%, they push you forward by 10%, resulting in a 20% improvement in effectiveness. You will also win back some of the supporters who may have unwittingly been following a dissident. Recognise and reward those who raise their motivation and move the others on.

You will always be left with some dissidents and downbeats. Remove them promptly – kindly and with resonance, but they have to go. They will probably be happier elsewhere, anyway. If you don't act, you will be legitimising dissidence and it will spread. People will assume that you are not serious about the strategies and cultures you purport to stand for. You will ruin your reputation and lose people's followership.

This isn't a philosophical position; I've seen companies follow the advice, and others that have not done so. Without exception, the former companies have done better in achieving their targets.

A TALE OF TWO LEADERSHIPS

A few years ago, I took on two new clients; each was keen to initiate a resonant leadership culture. In both cases, I ended up working intensively for several months with members of the board, and we identified a significant minority of dissidents on the board.

In organisation A, the chief executive acted decisively and fired his dissident directors. His organisation went on to achieve its three-year goals within twenty-six months. In organisation B, the leadership was slow to accept the need to get rid of anybody; eventually they shed a few second- and third-tier dissidents, but for poor performance rather than dissidence, and they did not tackle dissidence within the board. Inevitably the organisation's performance plummeted.

Dealing with the intractable dissidents is a key part of courageous accountability, not least because you have a responsibility to the greater good of all employees and shareholders. But you still need to deal with them in a way that doesn't compromise the culture of resonance in your organisation. This entails making it clear that you are not taking punitive action; rather, you have given them opportunities (not threats or ultimata) to align themselves with the culture, but as they have not chosen to do so, it is your duty to help them find a place in which they will be able to thrive.

Some dissident archetypes

The classic naysayers are easy to spot, but there are some less obviously dissident archetypes I still encounter regularly. You may have come across them yourself:

- **Above it all:** often senior people who only see the need for zest in those junior to themselves. They regard their elevated position as either proof that they are already perfect or meaning they are exempt. Fortunately above-it-alls are dying out, just like the other dodos.
- **Know it all:** individuals who fail to grasp that they are not implementing the knowledge or values they champion. Their noses are often out of joint because the knowledge that once made them feel special is now everybody's. They may

even be feeling insecure about other people being better at it than them.

- **I'm all right, Jack:** people who sacrifice long-term results on the altar of short-term self-interest. This works for them, because they intend to be gone long before the chickens come home to roost.

- **Smiling cynic:** classic cases of talking without walking. They have learned to wear a zest mask and think they are fooling us about their inner negativity. They aren't. They are also frequently above-it-alls – a dangerous combination.

- **Good enough:** high achievers despite their rejection of positivity and optimism. Clearly talented, they regard their personal success as proof that the benefits of zest are fictitious and refuse to consider the abundance of evidence to the contrary. These flat-earthers often fail to understand their dissatisfaction with life, but it is actually a direct result of their not aiming towards their full potential.

These archetypes may be more subtle in how they convey dissidence, but they are toxic nonetheless.

Leadership stress

Manifesting resonant leadership values consistently under pressure can mean making far-reaching changes to our mindset and behaviour to build leadership resilience. Such personal change need no longer be elusive, patchy or short-lived, thanks to the spectacular developments in our understanding of the psychology of change.

Leadership resilience is about more than eating pressure for breakfast; it's about keeping it together when stuff hits the fan, and this is the leadership challenge I hear most about from:

- Subordinates who are feeling aggrieved at the high-handed, callous or self-interested behaviour of their boss
- Managers who are frustrated by their lack of ability to continue treating people well when things get intense and they feel under pressure
- Chief executives who are puzzled by poor engagement data despite the company values being about respect, inclusion and valuing others

But there is hope. The lack of behavioural and/or emotional stability, often inaccurately labelled as reverting to type, stems from flawed behavioural change strategies. Surprisingly, leadership resilience is largely a learned behaviour, rather than simply genetic, so people can correct a deficit in resilience if they approach it in the right way.

As we have seen, willpower isn't the answer, and not knowing that fact is a major obstacle to leaders mastering these issues. Using willpower to hold it together under pressure is always going to fail if our unconscious mind is programmed to allow us to lose resonance when stressed. As we saw in Chapter 1, it seems that this is the case for most of us.

Willpower can only override our default responses to situations if we have enough mental bandwidth available – and then only briefly and never in extreme cases. Even quite low levels of pressure can consume all our mental bandwidth. When that happens, our default traits emerge, and for most of us that means getting dissonant (ie impacting others' emotional states negatively).

I'm sure we all know the feeling: if we're caught between a deadline and a report who is frustrating us, our courtesy and respect can soon wear thin. But the costs of such lapses into dissonance are huge:

- Engagement is damaged or destroyed as reports withdraw their followership.

- Discretionary effort is withheld and productivity falls sharply.

- Costs rise and/or revenue slows, and/or growth slackens.

- People vote with their feet – good people don't tolerate leadership dissonance for long.

Most tellingly, in leadership terms, behaving resonantly 97% of the time is pointless if a person behaves dissonantly 3% of the time, for two reasons:

- Their reports are never sure which version of them has turned up today.

- Negative events have a much more powerful effect on people than positive ones, because we are genetically programmed to focus on negative events as a matter of survival and to take positive events for granted.

Let's be honest, that 97% thing is *really* common.

A decade after starting work on researching resonant leadership, Boyatzis and McKee returned to re-interview the individuals who'd been best at it. They found that the vast majority of them had reverted to a dissonant leadership style and put the reversal down to leadership stress: the special pressure leaders feel because of the demands of power and of being in the limelight. There's no place for them to hide. Their financial performance is there for everyone to see and their head is likely to be the first to roll if it disappoints. Moreover, the approachability that characterises their resonance means they are always much more visible to those they lead than an autocrat would be.[28]

---

28 R Boyatzis and A McKee, *Resonant Leadership: Renewing yourself and connecting with others through mindfulness, hope and compassion* (Harvard Business School Press, 2005)

Fortunately we can learn from how the minority of leaders who sustained resonant leadership for more than a decade did it. And it had absolutely nothing to do with willpower. It turns out they all had some way of counteracting the negative programming impact of leadership stress on their behaviour. They regularly included in their routine activities that provided positive psychological conditioning to neutralise the damaging impact of leadership stress. By now, you may recognise this as a cognitive behavioural approach.

I see the same phenomenon in surveys of former delegates to courses run by my company, New Impetus International. There's a concrete statistical relationship between how much our alumni put into actively managing their psychology and the scale of improvement they report in their professional performance (and in their personal lives).

Eating pressure for breakfast needs to become an unconscious routine rather than a macho expression of bravado and hope. That comes from achieving deep psychological resilience, which in turn requires active management of the psychological environment.

Positive psychology research in recent years has proved that we build resilience when we spend time in positive emotional states. When we experience positive emotion, we are constantly triggering the chemical and synaptic changes in our brain that manifest as increased ability to push through challenges, navigate setbacks without losing momentum, and survive stressful and even traumatic experiences. Indeed, resilience has been shown to determine whether we experience post-traumatic growth or stress disorder. That is the reason the US Army has, since 2009, trained all its non-commissioned officers as positive psychology coaches, under the auspices of Professor Martin Seligman. Substance abuse, depression, post-traumatic stress disorder and panic symptoms among troops have since been halved.

The benefits extend beyond leadership behaviour into all aspects of personal effectiveness. High levels of stress wipe out clarity of thinking, creativity, EI, analytical reasoning, motivation and energy – and feel unpleasant. The health dangers of prolonged stress are well documented and can be extreme. Highly resilient people avoid these damaging states more often than others. Even in heavily pressured situations, they spend more time in high-performance states and so, as the data clearly shows,[29] they outperform others – and enjoy life more.

Lastly, in psychological terms it makes no sense to try and reverse dissonance and performance collapse once they've kicked in. This is not because the thinking behind wanting to put things right isn't appropriate, but because, sadly, it's already too late: no amount of willpower and strength of character can enable the brain to achieve that. The cortex, or

---

29 Lyubomirsky et al, The benefits of frequent positive affect

part of the brain where our higher functions reside (including intellect, EI, creativity), is closed down by a combination of the limbic system and the pre-frontal cortex when we experience an emotional hijack. In simple terms, the kit we need for higher functioning is temporarily and comprehensively put into standby mode. Furthermore, the hormones generated by the emotional flooding that stress creates can take eight hours to dissipate from the system, and for the whole of that time our performance and behaviour are impacted negatively.

Profit impact of leadership resonance

The answer is to focus on creating a positively conditioning psychological environment that will build resilience. The evidence is clear: this is the only approach that works.

Again, it's Professor Richard Boyatzis who, in the unpublished 1999 paper *Developing Emotional Intelligence*, has provided us with evidence of the impact of resonance. An initial study he conducted had indicated that the most important impact a leader has on their organisation is the emotional climate that they create within the organisation, so the next step was to quantify the impact. He and his team looked at a cluster of chief executive qualities to make a comparative assessment of their impact: high intelligence, relationship skills, and a combination of diligence and resonance. This is what they found:

- CEOs who were skilled at building and managing relationships increased average profits by 110%.

- CEOs who demonstrated a combination of diligence and resonance achieved 490% of the profit of the average CEO.

What the figures demonstrate is that effective relationship management on its own is not enough. So what lies behind these startling results? The mechanism that drives the surge in profitability is discretionary effort, and we'll explore this phenomenon in detail in the next chapter.

NINE
Releasing Discretionary Effort

If discretionary effort is the key to greater profitability, how can you generate a critical mass of it in your organisation? Only from high levels of emotional engagement that see staff contributing to their maximum potential while still being keen to develop and improve. There is often pressure from stakeholders, shareholders, parent companies etc on leaders to produce good engagement scores. HR departments are tasked with measuring and, if necessary, improving these scores. There are countless proprietary engagement surveys out there, assessing everything from what people think of their recreational facilities to whether they tell their friends that theirs is a good place to work. Building the sort of emotional engagement that releases discretionary effort, though, is about far more than good survey scores.

Investing in what matters

In most organisations, the vast majority of people are disengaged. Global surveys of engagement across the Western world reveal broadly consistent statistics:

- 10–15% are highly engaged
- 20–25% are actively disengaged
- 60–70% are passively disengaged

The 60–70% majority, who are passively disengaged, are neither happy nor unhappy. They turn up and do a good enough job, but it doesn't excite them and they don't feel any particular attachment to the organisation. Their discretionary effort is low at best. Most CEOs would acknowledge that this reflects their organisation.

My view is that you need to get rid of the actively disengaged and work hard to win the engagement of the passive mass. But how best to do that? If you offer a passively disengaged person a wellbeing initiative that's all about recreational facilities and healthy eating in the canteen, it's not actually going to make a big difference. To the sceptical wing of the disengaged, such efforts look shallow and insincere. They might generate a few more ticks in the annual survey, but they won't win you much in the way of genuine emotional engagement.

Inspiring emotional engagement is not something that can be achieved through implementing a one-size-fits-all approach overseen by HR alone. These specialists are invaluable when it comes to understanding and introducing employment policies that the majority of staff will appreciate, such as flexible working hours, opportunities for enhancing skills, etc, but their department's work has to be complemented by the personal efforts of the leadership and line management. Only they can win deep emotional engagement through projecting the integrity of the organisation and creating an environment where colleagues predominantly experience positive emotions at work.

When I started looking into the relationship between engagement and discretionary effort, I found a mismatch between what engagement surveys measure and those aspects of engagement that drive high discretionary effort. The senior leadership of any organisation needs to have an accurate assessment of the level of emotional engagement of their intermediate leaders and colleagues, because that's what will define the level of discretionary effort throughout their organisation.

The leaders of the companies that bring New Impetus in know that there is more to engagement than nice-looking scores. They realise that there is more financial performance potential in their organisation only if their engagement scores reflect a genuine sense of attachment, and that their ability to attract and retain talent relies on the perception that their workforce finds their organisation a rewarding place to work.

What characterises deep emotional engagement with an organisation? It's when people feel a warm connection with the organisation and a fondness for the conspicuous figures in it. They say things like 'I just love it here. It's the best job I've ever had.' They have high-quality relationships with their colleagues and those who lead and supervise them. They may even have a fulfilling social life based on friendship groups that spring up at work. They feel respected and well treated.

Part of all that comes from the awareness that they are themselves making an important contribution to the organisation. They understand how that contribution fits into the overall vision. What's more, they feel that by working to achieve the organisation's goals, they will also be achieving their own personal goals, creating a future for themselves in the organisation they love or in a career they find rewarding.

When someone finds that level of alignment and sense of belonging in their work, they will spontaneously go beyond what is strictly necessary for them to do their jobs.

Discretionary effort

Discretionary effort is the effort that people put in over and above that required to meet targets, get a performance assessment of 'expected' and comply with organisational standards. Any level of effort beyond that is discretionary in that people don't have to put it in. They can choose how hard they're going to work at their job, and people usually do so, whether they're conscious of it or not, on the basis of how they feel about the organisation.

This means that discretionary effort varies according to the expectations of the organisation. If you're expected to work hard for ten hours a day to be doing your job properly, the extra hours beyond the average working day are not discretionary. If you're expected to turn up and work hard for eight hours, then being present for ten hours but only working hard for eight of them is not discretionary effort, it's presenteeism.

Character effort

While engagement with the organisation encourages discretionary effort, it's worth noting that some people will put in discretionary effort because that's just who they are. This is character effort. Even though they may work in an organisation with low engagement scores, the standards they set themselves will drive them to put in extra effort. If these people contribute so much through their personally motivated character effort, just think how much more they'll offer when deep emotional engagement with their organisation activates a further band of discretionary effort, one that is motivated externally. A leader's job is to recruit for character effort and cultivate engagement-based discretionary effort.

Impact on revenue and profit

The way discretionary effort works is that it drives improvement across all the measures that contribute to financial and operational success. It engenders respect for company resources, both human and physical, with material impact on costs. It has a major impact by boosting productivity – some sources quote by 30%.

You can see it at work when someone who feels mildly unwell decides to go into the office so as not to let down their colleagues or to complete a task that is due, rather than staying at home. You can see it in the productivity of the person working from home who is using the relative peace and quiet to shift a lot of work rather than getting side-tracked by domestic tasks. These increases in productivity are translated into higher output, reductions in costs, more time spent in business expansion and pursuit of new sales, and less time spent on non-productive activity (not all down time is non-productive, of course).

SLOW OFF THE MARK

The CEO of an advertising company that was having a bad quarter called in her senior team and encouraged them to spend the next two hours on the phone generating business. After two hours, she had done her stint and was particularly impressed with how one of her directors had got on.

When she went to check on progress elsewhere, though, she was disappointed. She found another director sliding a piece of folded tissue between the keys of his keyboard.

'If I'm going to put in this big effort,' he explained, 'I want everything to be just so. So I've cleaned the keyboard, I've cleared my desk area and I've designed a reply form. Look, I've printed it out so that every time I make a call, I can put the key data in the top, and then I can fill in the rest and that will make it easier to capture the details. I'm almost ready to go.'

All this had taken most of the two hours assigned to the task. In fact, this displacement activity was the opposite of discretionary effort.

Avoidant or displacement behaviour is less likely to happen when people feel that they would be letting themselves and their colleagues down if they didn't act promptly and decisively. Engaged people have more respect for all company resources: energy, materials, time, costs.

A discretionary increase in productivity, efficiency and effectiveness represents, to use an accounting term, marginal, ie incremental, effort. There is little or no additional cost attached to it, so nearly all of the marginal income is in effect marginal profit, flowing directly to the bottom line. My observation is that high levels of discretionary effort distinguish winning organisations from the rest. The level of discretionary effort in the world's most prestigious accounting, legal and tech firms is remarkable, which seems to bear out my theory.

Generating extra profits of itself is not enough; leaders have to share the benefits derived from having a highly engaged workforce across the organisation. If an organisation prioritises earning vast sums to distribute to its shareholders, or has a big boss earning £30m a year (more than a thousand times more than the average person in the organisation), it will crush engagement.

THE TURNAROUND

Fifteen years ago, a global professional services company was revelling in its status as a major player. Everybody in the firm was highly capable and it only hired the brightest and the best. The employees' self-concept was one of international excellence, and they attached great importance to it.

One of the company's competitors had been working with a large employer to address its challenges with IT system resilience. The consultants had not been able to resolve the challenges; in fact, they had got worse. Our major player rode up on its white charger to fix the mess and found that it wasn't able to do so. It did sort things out in the end, but not within the expected timescale, and not before it became associated with a major failure. The scandal was such that the company plummeted from being the number-one employer of choice to almost the bottom of the list. Not surprisingly, its engagement scores collapsed from around 70% to scores down in the thirties.

It was at this point that I was invited in to work on engagement by the company's enlightened managing director. He was committed to positivity and to treating people well, and was intelligent, hard-working and likeable. Within a year, the engagement scores had risen to the high sixties – we had literally doubled them.

This should have been the end of the story, but sadly, within two years, this MD was replaced by a fellow board member who was somewhat blinded by his own intellectual brilliance and had little regard even for his fellow leaders. I'll leave you to guess what happened to the engagement scores then.

Discretionary effort cuts both ways

Discretionary effort covers a wide range of activity that varies according to your role in the organisation. It's not simply about working hard, perfecting your output, increasing your sales and streamlining your operating costs, especially if you are a leader. You need to be seen to be exercising discretionary effort, not only to set a good example, but to meet the standards required to win the followership of those you are responsible for leading. Discretionary effort in that context can mean being prepared to act on hard, painful-to-implement decisions.

I have seen great leadership cultures brought low by two or three senior leaders withholding their discretionary effort. It wasn't that they didn't work hard; rather they didn't sustain their efforts to improve their resilience and ended up reverting to counter-cultural behaviour under pressure. This was then compounded by the CEO failing to grasp the nettle and remove them, perhaps for fear of losing their experience and skills, or simply because they couldn't find within themselves the grit to hold these cultural dissidents to account. In every one of these cases, employee engagement collapsed as trust in leadership evaporated. You can't expect staff to trust you if you tolerate in senior leaders the behaviour you're trying to eliminate in more junior people. Ultimately, financial performance suffered as discretionary effort across the organisations withered and talent walked.

Allowing dissident leadership to remain in place can do even worse than signal weakness, low commitment or insincerity; it can spawn factions. When you have two groups of leaders opposing each other, they will begin to canvass support and recruit allies, placing pressure on their senior reports to take sides. Managers can be traumatised by such conflicts, worried by the impact of negative internal politics on both the organisation and their career. All the energy that could be driving greater productivity and other improvements is being dissipated on in-fighting and corporate handwringing.

Where the CEO acts courageously to nip dissident leadership in the bud, their uncompromising commitment to the principles and values the leadership expects everyone to adopt has a transformational impact. With a highly engaged workforce around them, they are well on the way to developing an emancipated high-profits ethos in their organisation.

The next chapter outlines how you can initiate this radical, positive change.

TEN

Ethos Change For Exceptional Outcomes

Getting culture right belongs near the top of every chief executive's priorities. Think of how Apple's fortunes varied depending on whether Steve Jobs was in place or not. Think of Bill Gates and now Satya Nadella at Microsoft, Larry Page and Sergey Brin at Google, Jeff Bezos at Amazon, Mark Zuckerberg at Facebook, Elon Musk at Tesla. More than championing culture, they own it.

If there is nothing more important than the culture of an organisation, how is it that there is such widespread scepticism about culture change? So many people have seen serial initiative failure in this context that it's not surprising their expectations are low, but it doesn't have to be that way. Addressing these three challenges will transform the probability of success:

- Empathy and resonance:
  - Teams leading culture change are easily perceived as an elite, which may prevent them from resonating with the colleagues they are trying to influence.
  - Beware of change leaders who signal their belief in their own superior insight. They need to be able to show that they can see change from others' points of view and understand how they feel about it.
- Authenticity:
  - People are acutely aware of the inherent hypocrisy in initiatives that seek to install a bottom-up culture in a top-down way, and as a result they don't trust them. Unless the target values are visible in the boardroom, you will not get buy-in.
  - Successful leadership culture change initiatives have one thing in common: the man or woman at the top is committed enough to expose their own behaviour to scrutiny. They may not have been exemplars from day one, but they publicly addressed the changes they themselves needed to make.

- Values statements are merely a cultural *aspiration*. There is a world of difference between the behaviours we aspire to and those we manifest. An organisation's culture is how people *actually* behave, and people evaluate their organisation based on that.

- Meaningful consultation:
  - Sham consultation fools no one and fuels resentment. Don't agree a new culture at board/group HQ before seeking wider input.
  - Consultation must involve asking, listening and responding, and where necessary explaining why certain demands cannot be met, or it does infinitely more harm than good.

Leadership, engagement and culture: interlocking facets

A 'gestalt' is an organised whole that is more than the sum of its parts, and the three elements of leadership, engagement and culture together definitely constitute a gestalt. I call it ethos.

Even if people perceive this, they tend to think of leadership as a top manager/high potentials issue, engagement as an employee issue and culture as something else altogether. In fact, it's not uncommon for the three areas to be addressed in different years by different teams and treated as independent initiatives.

If these initiatives are handled out of house, they may be undertaken by third parties that advise only on the area of their speciality, resulting in even more of a silo approach.

If we meld the three strands into their natural whole, we have the chance to release huge untapped financial potential by going beyond empowerment all the way to emancipation. To achieve this, we need to look further than purely skills-based leadership development and engagement programmes that overemphasise measurement and standardised metrics. Similarly, we need to design cultural interventions that do more than focus on communicating aspirational behaviours, standards and values.

Top leaders have the perspective, breadth of view and awareness of the interplay between resource and results to treat these three facets as part of a whole. Delegating responsibility for ethos change to a level where people do not have a day-to-day strategic overview of the organisation's activity is never going to enable a gestalt approach.

Leaders are as leaders do

Most leadership interventions focus on skills: strategy, decision making, influencing, goal setting, etc. Little emphasis is placed on leaders' cultural impact and responsibility, and even less on the fact that engagement levels respond directly to leaders' behaviour.

Rarer still is the intervention aimed at encouraging leaders to overcome learned helplessness and refrain from being judgemental about employee mindset.

Leadership behaviour sets the standards that people copy and reveals much more about what stakeholders actually value (or will tacitly accept) than posters and slogans. Humans are smart; they know that actions are a mirror of the soul, but words are an unreliable information source. Most of the time behaviour comes from the unconscious and is true to our self-concept; most of the time our words come from the conscious and can be manipulated.

Even good leaders routinely underestimate the need to see themselves as cultural icons. It can also be hard for them to accept that their behaviour tells people everything about how seriously they buy into corporate value aspirations. Engagement is affected more by leadership behaviour than by just about anything else because employees react to what leaders actually do above what they say, and this is *especially* true when stuff is hitting the fan. In my experience, 2–3% dissonant behaviour negates 97–98% resonance.

PREACHING BUT NOT PRACTISING

One of the top ten consulting companies in Europe was renowned for its people-valuing culture, chiefly because it made bold statements about how important it was for the organisation to treat its workforce with respect, give them the autonomy to act and look after them. Unfortunately, it refused to commit to any initiatives to ensure that senior managers conducted themselves in alignment with the culture that they were championing. When it came down to it, the partners in charge were not interested in change; they were simply interested in continuing to make money in the way they had always done. The initiative floundered and disengagement gathered momentum.

Lack of understanding, fear of change and laziness often give rise to the perception that there is a conflict between treating people well and making money.

In most companies, those below the highest level of leadership have limited power to secure collaboration from overloaded or reluctant individuals who are substantially more senior than themselves. Delegating to a level of seniority where people have a challenge gaining traction on the issues is misguided: the initiative is compromised from day one.

Remember the substance

In my experience, cultural initiatives are often incomplete. They focus on messaging the values through expensive workshops with high-concept videos, great training experiences and lovely awaydays, but then no one follows up by overhauling the whole process of assessing people's performance and rewarding them accordingly. Claiming to value your people and treat them with respect must be backed up with practical action.

Across the seniority grades, your company needs to review, refine and rebalance scores of target behaviours against which individuals are measured. The complexity and scale of the task demonstrate how important it is and how extensive the benefits to be gained from making sure that the fundamental process of developing people is carried out in alignment with the culture you want to promote. On top of this, the organisation's learning and development programme will need to be reviewed and internal training courses re-written. External partners' content should be included and new partners appointed where necessary.

The investment demanded by such an undertaking means that it can fall foul of short-sighted cost-benefit analysis. The term 'cost-benefit' is inherently pessimistic priming, automatically conjuring up a negative evaluation; far better to undertake an investment-benefit analysis.

The other aspect of such a comprehensive overhaul of organisational culture is that it's not quick. It's hard to imagine a leadership team or a chief executive that would give the go-ahead to a project on this scale without knowing when they could expect to see an ROI. An optimistic assessment would probably conclude that half of the benefits might come quite quickly, but the other half might take a year or two.

Chief executives are often vulnerable to their shareholders' and the market's preference for short-term results. As a result, investing in any programme that is going to take two years to deliver a return calls for a strong heart and powerfully convincing arguments. The rewards of doing so are exceptional.

A phased approach

The pragmatic approach is to address all the elements at the same time, but in phases. Doing leadership, engagement and culture change sequentially never works, because two out of the three elements will, at best, be trailing behind the one you are focusing on in any given year. At worst, they will be undermining what you are trying to do in the area for development.

If the aim is to address all three areas in one year, a good starting point is to train leaders, managers and supervisors in the desired cultural behaviours to ensure alignment with your aspirational leadership values. At this stage, it is important to give as wide a range of colleagues as is operationally feasible an overview of the nature and aims of the programme. Complement this with a high-level review of the key performance indicators and behaviours that people are assessed against, and of reward and recognition policies.

Setting off on the path to culture change in this highly visible, pragmatic way gains some initial traction, especially if it is accompanied by any required re-education of top leadership. Seeing the changes in senior people and in processes will stimulate an appetite for the initiative that helps with embedding the change more deeply and broadly in the following year. The first year's programme can then be cascaded throughout the organisation by the people who participated in year one.

Having said all that, by far the most effective solution is to do a comprehensive overhaul in one year. Among New Impetus client organisations that recently did this is a leadership team that was targeted by its group to turn their business around in three years. They achieved this in just over two.

TOP TIPS TO CRACK CULTURE CHANGE

The key actions below summarise my lessons learned from twenty-four years of cementing new cultures. All of them deserve emphasis because they are arbiters of success.

Long cuts:

- Buy-in works, imposition fails. It takes time to respectfully build buy-in, but the more effort you put in here, the more certain you can be of success.

- Explain the outcomes delta – ie the contrast between the benefits of change and the penalties of stasis – to as many people as you can.
- Be ready to change your plans through consulting widely and listening to opinions. Don't confuse spinning the old plan harder with adjusting to a new plan.
- Tell the truth. Be open about why this initiative is going to be different, both in terms of effectiveness and leadership commitment. If you can't do this (because it isn't going to be different), you need to ask yourself why you're doing it.
- Change everything, because unless product brochures, KPIs, personal-development plans, appraisal criteria, organisational structures and so on all reflect the new way, people will disengage.
- Keep going. Successful culture change is the result of countless small changes persistently applied and the sum of those behavioural and thinking changes in every individual in the business. Remember, organisational change moves in waves that are more like several Severn bores than a single tsunami.

Short cuts:

- Convert sceptics, fire dissidents. No one likes firing people, but as they threaten everyone else's future, you need to fire dissidents (see chapter 8) early, or people will question your commitment. While dissidents and downbeats remain, they slow down or even derail change.
- Foster ownership. Focus people on their own change, not on other people's. If everyone is waiting for their neighbour or boss to change first, or if they use others' minor failures as a reason not to try themselves, they're hampering progress right from the start.
- Invest more in change training than in communication. If people get it, they'll recognise the need for change as much as you do. If they don't, you've either failed to win them over (see the earlier point about buy-in) or their attempts at personal behavioural change are not working, or haven't even started, because they don't believe they can change.
- Invest in training people *how* to change. Willpower isn't the secret; cognitive behavioural conditioning is. Humans only ever change by making adjustments to their unconscious. It's a lot simpler than it sounds and it always delivers.

Beyond empowerment to emancipation

An enlightened corporate ethos creates resilient businesses that deliver superior returns for shareholders, employers, partners and customers. But however hard you work with the leadership of an organisation, reaching beyond it to address the culture, you will not be able to engage the majority and harness their contribution if they don't feel love for their organisation. If people's confidence in it and in the ability of its leadership to change is low, it will be heading for initiative failure. What's the point of supporting a change initiative if people think it will fail, and there's going to be yet another one just around the corner?

What if there wasn't an artificial barrier between those who are leaders and those who aren't? Retired US Navy Captain David Marquet has an approach he calls 'leader-leader': everybody at all levels in an organisation is a leader.[30] He baulks at the idea that people in organisations only have the power to act if it is given to them by their bosses. He calls that sort of culture 'leader-follower': a set-up in which leaders take all the decisions and followers just do as they're told. 'Don't empower, emancipate' is his mantra.

Are your people showing less initiative than you'd like? Are they so afraid to act without permission

---

[30] LD Marquet, *Turn the Ship Around!* (Portfolio/Penguin, 2012)

that if their boss is not there, things don't get done? This can happen when an organisation's attempts to empower people inadvertently reinforce the message that they only have power to act because their boss gives it to them. People end up feeling that they don't have permission to act at all – if their boss has given it, they can just as easily take it away again. In this situation, there is no universal right to take action; it's just not in the organisation's DNA.

HOW TO SCUPPER AN INITIATIVE

I remember working on a cultural initiative with the UK CEO of a global pharma company. He was explaining to his extended management team what the new values meant in practice. I'll never forget him walking up to the screen on which one of the new values, 'Licence to make mistakes', was being projected. He placed his hand over the second s in the word 'mistakes' while turning and literally glaring at the room and saying, 'Clear?'

It was indeed clear – and the values initiative collapsed right there. This company became one of the many organisations I know of where the senior middle management and below show admirably resonant leadership values in their behaviour, the impact of which is undermined by C-suite members who think they are above it all. Unless the target values manifest in the boardroom, no one will respect leadership's motives.

Crossing the chasm

Not everyone is equally predisposed to adopting a new culture or empowerment ethos. You may be more familiar with this model as it applies to new technology, but the five adopter groups are the same:

- **Innovators** jump right in – they probably had a hand in creating the new initiative.

- **Early adopters** are adventurous and often enjoy change for its own sake, so they come on board quickly and are happy to take quite a lot on trust.

These two groups probably represent less than 20% of our companies' population. What we are really interested in is the next two groups, who represent the vast majority:

- **Early majority:** they are open to change once they've heard the full argument, and can be active in influencing others

- **Late majority:** they are less active and more conservative

The challenge we have is the gap between early adopters and the early majority – what George Moore calls the chasm.[31] It results from the conservative early majority being more sceptical than early adopters. They

---

[31] GA Moore, *Crossing the Chasm* (Harper Business Essentials, 1991, 1999, 2014)

need further information, perhaps even a complete business case, before they get on board.

If you're stuck in the chasm, take a look at your messaging and its information content. Go back to talking more about the 'why' than the 'how' of the projected change.

Once the early majority is on board, the late majority will follow. They will be persuaded by the same information, just more slowly, so long as you maintain consistency in your messaging.

The final group, known as **laggards** or **phobics**, may never fully come on board. These will probably be 5–20% of the people you are concerned with. If you have a substantial laggard group, you may need an external intervention to change their mindset.

Talent – how to get it, hone it and keep it

A human being is basically a brain. I know it feels more as if we are a body, because so much of life is about sensation, but the truth is that all of our experiences, emotions, drives and motivations, hopes and fears, memories and goals – our sensations as well, come to that – live in the brain. It's not too much of a stretch to think of our body as a receptacle that exists simply to transport, feed, protect and reproduce future generations of brains that include our DNA.

Why am I asking you to think about the brain in the context of talent? Because so much of getting it right with talent depends on nurturing the psychology of the talent you wish to attract, develop and retain. This has a far greater impact than anything else you can do.

Uncovering talent

Finding and uncovering talent is about releasing latent potential. Most humans operate at a level far below what they are truly capable of. Our unnecessarily limited ideas about what we can achieve trap us all beneath the glass ceiling of our self-belief. This is not because we lack courage or vision, or even because we consciously underestimate our own worth. It is an unconscious process that results from life experiences teaching us that we sometimes – perhaps often – don't get the outcomes we were hoping for. No amount of striving, wanting, willpower and goal setting will enable us to exceed our unconscious limiting beliefs, except perhaps briefly.

Releasing latent potential begins with individuals grasping intellectually and emotionally that they are genuinely capable of more than they may think. There are plenty of examples in our shared experience and culture to win this argument. Sometimes all it takes is to remind people of their friends and colleagues in whom they personally see more capability than those people see in themselves, and then pointing out that they are exactly the same. It's then a relatively simple step to teach them how to replace their limiting beliefs with enabling self-knowledge that more accurately describes their true potential. This is the process of cognitive restructuring I described in Chapter 5.

There are many benefits to people getting closer to their true potential. Anything that improves individual performance is clearly good for the employer, but it's equally good for the person concerned. The sense of achievement, coupled with growing confidence in their ability, is transformational.

Anyone who works for an employer who gives them such a life-enhancing experience is indeed fortunate. Such people become enthusiastic ambassadors, and their evangelising about the firm can only attract other talented people.

Honing talent

Over the past thirty years, research has repeatedly shown that the most important workplace skill is EI – defined as the ability to understand and manage one's shifting emotions and to have insight into the viewpoints and emotions of other people, with a view to regulating one's own impact on them. EI adds value and enhances performance; it's the most significant factor in leadership effectiveness and the learnable skill that delivers improved teamwork, followership, influencing and selling.

The key word in the last paragraph is 'learnable'. A lot of EI training focuses on behaviour. Though this unquestionably adds value, it may not address a fundamental point. Of the two targets of EI, self and others, the latter is by far the more challenging to deal with effectively. We must learn to focus on others not just when things are going well, but when we are facing adverse circumstances.

In difficult times, human beings automatically and unconsciously centre their awareness upon themselves and lose the focus on others that is essential for displaying EI. Avoiding this inbuilt vulnerability requires us to build both resilience and high self-esteem (see Chapter 2), so any interventions that boost those two qualities will add huge amounts of perceived value.

Retaining talent

A Gallup Organization study of two million employees at 700 companies established that the supervisor relationship is the key factor in determining how long an employee stays with their employer.[32] Technological advances in digitalisation and communication in

---

32 A Zipkin, The wisdom of thoughtfulness. *New York Times* (31 May 2000) section C, pp1, 10

recent years have led to a situation in which the job market is more mobile than ever before. Information about employers (including your company) and multiple attractive job opportunities are all highly visible online through social media and recruitment platforms. Talented people can be more choosy and less tolerant of circumstances they think can be improved on.

Regardless of what is driving this, we need to react to the facts of the situation. Retaining talent goes far beyond creating an appealing workplace environment and offering attractive benefits and wellbeing programmes. It's much more important that people feel respected and valued, so the behaviour of supervisors and managers with responsibility for leading talented employees is critical.

In my experience, the majority of leaders – but not all – understand this well. The leaders' behaviour, particularly when an organisation is facing extreme stress or adverse conditions, must retain at its core the respect and Grace people now expect in the workplace. And the responsibility for treating others well extends beyond leaders across the entire organisation. People are sensitive to the pervasive culture of an organisation, and no one is going to choose a critical or negative emotional climate over a positive and supportive one if they have the option.

Most organisations aspire to having an enlightened and caring business culture. We have to go further. The full potential of a corporation for superior profit and aspirational wellbeing can only be reliably realised by simultaneously addressing all three aspects of the ethos for exceptional outcomes: cultural values, leadership behaviour and deep emotional engagement.

Conclusion

You may feel it's been something of an epic journey from the behaviour of infinitesimally small structures of the brain to the boardrooms of multinational companies. I hope that what stays with you is a well-founded belief in the possibility of positive change delivering superior profits and inspirational wellbeing in synergy.

On testing days, leadership can seem a daunting adventure: not enough opportunities for creative thinking and daring strategy, and too much time spent providing answers and solutions that others should be capable of finding for themselves. Too much firefighting and summoning up gargantuan last-minute efforts to beat targets and deadlines. Too much balancing the often-conflicting demands of shareholders, customers, employees, intermediate leaders, talent, press and pundits.

Yet these are precisely the occasions when leaders can display their resonance. 'Out of touch' is the damning charge the press and public level at leaders in business, politics and the public sector. If you can get 'in touch' with your reports, the wider staff and all your stakeholders, and resonate with them, the rest – be it sales, partnerships or industrial relations – becomes so much easier and more successful.

And it doesn't stop there. I've cited the compelling evidence in terms of EBITDA, and equally your family and friends will share in the benefits of your Grace. All of your relationships flourish more readily when they are full of resonance.

Throughout the book, you will have seen tips, suggestions and exercises to get you as a leader started on a personal journey of further improvement, and even transformation: incremental changes that you can incorporate into your busy schedule as effective ways of accelerating the change. If what you need right now is wholesale organisational change, please go right ahead and find out what New Impetus has to offer by visiting our website: www.newimpetus.com.

Having read this book, you're probably feeling eager to put its techniques into practise. Hold hard to that thought and turn it into immediate action. Don't let this be a business book you get excited about for a while, then drift away from. That's the way the old dominant neurites make you behave. Please, seize the day, take decisive action, exploit the personal and competitive advantage this new science offers. I don't mind what you do – obviously I'd be delighted if you'd like my company to be part of it, but in any event, for your own sake, act fast. If you do one thing towards implementation now, even a small thing, you are 40% more likely to follow through.

I wish you every success in everything you work to achieve.

References

Achor, S, *The Happiness Advantage: The seven principles of positive psychology that fuel success and performance at work* (Crown Publishing Group, 2010)

Bargh, JA, Chen, M and Burrows, L, Automaticity of social behavior: Direct effects of trait construct and stereotype activation on action. *Journal of Personality and Social Psychology*, *71* (1996), pp230–244

Boyatzis, R, Developing Emotional Intelligence [unpublished paper] (Case Western Reserve University, Department of Organizational Behavior, 1999)

Boyatzis, R and McKee, A, *Resonant Leadership: Renewing yourself and connecting with others through mindfulness, hope and compassion* (Harvard Business Review, 2005)

Chabris, C and Simons, D, *The Invisible Gorilla: And other ways our intuitions deceive us* (Crown Publishing Group, 2010)

Cherniss, C and Goleman D, *Competency Study Database* (Hay/McBer, 1997)

Cherniss, C and Goleman, D, *The Emotionally Intelligent Workplace: How to select for, measure, and improve emotional intelligence in individuals, groups, and organizations* (Jossey-Bass, 2001)

Dijksterhuis, A, Think different: The merits of unconscious thought in preference development and decision making. *Journal of Personality and Social Psychology, 87:5* (2004), pp586–598

Duckworth, A, *Grit: The power of passion and perseverance* (Simon & Schuster, 2016)

Fredrickson, B, *Positivity: Groundbreaking research to release your inner optimist and thrive* (Crown Publishing Group, 2009)

Goleman, D, Boyatzis, R and McKee, A, *Primal Leadership: Realizing the power of emotional intelligence* (Harvard Business School Press, 2002)

REFERENCES

Green, T, Heinemann, S and Gusella, J, Molecular neurobiology and genetics: Investigation of neural function and dysfunction. *Neuron, 20:3* (1998), pp427–444

Helmstetter, S, *What to Say When You Talk to Your Self: Powerful new techniques to programme your potential success!* (Harper Collins, 1986)

Kahneman, D, *Thinking, Fast and Slow* (Allen Lane, 2011)

Kopelman, S, Rosette, AS and Thompson, L, The three faces of Eve: Strategic displays of positive, negative, and neutral emotions in negotiations. *Organizational Behavior and Human Decision Processes, 99:1* (2006), pp81–101

Kotulak, R, *Inside the Brain* (Andrews McMeel Publishing, 1996)

Kross, E, et al, Self-talk as a regulatory mechanism: How you do it matters. *Journal of Personality and Social Psychology, 106:2* (2014), pp304–324

Lyubomirsky, S, King, L, Diener, E and The Gallup Organization, The benefits of frequent positive affect: Does happiness lead to success? *Psychological Bulletin of the American Psychological Association, 131:6* (2005), pp803–855

Marquet, LD, *Turn the Ship Around!* (Portfolio/Penguin, 2012)

Moore, GA, *Crossing the Chasm: Marketing and selling disruptive products to mainstream customers* (Harper Business Essentials, 1991, 1999, 2014)

Orlick, T and Partington, J, Mental links to excellence. *The Sport Psychologist*, 2 (1988), pp105–130

Seligman, M, *Learned Optimism* (Knopf, 1991)

Seligman, M, *Authentic Happiness: Using the new positive psychology to realize your potential for lasting fulfillment* (Simon & Shuster, 2002)

Seligman, M, *Flourish: A new understanding of happiness and well-being – and how to achieve them* (Nicholas Brealey, 2011)

Sloan, S and Spencer, LM, Participant survey results. Hay Salesforce Effectiveness Seminar, Atlanta GA (Hay Group, 1991)

Zipkin, A, The wisdom of thoughtfulness. *New York Times*, 31 May 2000, section C, pp1, 10

Acknowledgements

I'd like to thank Katy Sands, my daughter, for her breath-taking talent, total commitment and unconditional love while building New Impetus International together for eighteen years. I'd literally be lost without you.

Lucy McCarraher, for teaching me her excellent approach to designing and writing a book, without which this would never have made it to the shelves. I'm forever indebted to her for her insight, friendship and warm leadership.

Verity Ridgman, for patiently and skilfully crafting readable words from my garrulous briefings and overly long drafts.

The Author

Graham Keen is a leading expert on business and personal potential, as well as an author, speaker and tutor. A business psychologist, former corporate finance adviser and CFO, he is CEO of New Impetus International, which he founded in 2000.

He studied with the father of positive psychology, Professor Martin Seligman, in 2003, to become one of the first five practising positive psychologists in the UK. Earlier, he was a senior manager advising entrepreneurs and major clients at Ernst & Young, and held three national and international CFO roles, before spending eight years as an independent corporate finance practitioner.

This unique combination of skills and experience gives him rare insight into business leaders' and owners' issues, motivations and opportunities, and how they can achieve personal happiness and business success in harmony.

His company has advised more than 250 businesses on embedding lasting positive change, and now works with entrepreneurs, private equity-backed companies, and complex international organisations across EMEA and beyond, delivering enlightened ethos and financial growth.

Contact

For information, video and audio resources, visit the New Impetus website: www.newimpetus.com.

You can find out more about Graham Keen on social media at:

in www.linkedin.com/in/grahamkeennewimpetus

@NewImpetus

@GKeenNewImpetus

To find out how your business performs in the key areas highlighted in this book, complete the performance culture scorecard at https://newimpetus.scoreapp.com.

Lightning Source UK Ltd.
Milton Keynes UK
UKHW011237220622
404802UK00009B/1934